the Process Equals the Product

"The work that [Dwayne] does and the vision that he has for youth is much needed for such a time as this especially in the city of Chicago. His pursuit to equip youth in every area of their lives for success is relentless! Dedication is one of his strengths as well as his ability to effectively communicate with the youth and relate to real life issues and deliver the "real talk"! …His formula works! My children and I are forever supporters of Dwayne and his endeavors…."

-Tasha Sykes

"[Dwayne's] passion, heart, compassion, resourcefulness, professionalism, and commanding presence is SECOND TO NONE. It is rare that you still meet a leader who develops teens with intentionality. The inspiration and far reaching impact he has in my life and the lives of countless others is unending. It has been my esteemed pleasure to know him and work with him to change the world, one teen at a time."

- Cicely V. Wilson

"After reading the beginning chapter of this book, it captivated me and prepared me to break all negative self talk to position my heart, mind, and soul to receive practical elements on how to find and live in purpose. It is a must read for anyone who is searching for their purpose, re-defineing their purpose, or affirming their purpose."

- Shameka Jones

"Mr. T. Dwayne Smith is the one person who has significantly influenced my life…. This gentleman has been my mentor since middle school. He is committed to changing the world one teen at a time by offering programs that equip and encourage. He has made a tremendous impact on my life providing me with countless opportunities to develop my leadership skills and utilize my gifts and talents to help other youth do the same. Through his guidance, I've discovered how important it is for all youth to have the same opportunities to be successful."

- Joshua Simmons

"Dwayne Smith has been a powerful and committed servant to God and has lived according to His purpose. He is the kind of man that gets things done and makes no excuses along the way! "The Process Equals the Product" is a book that inspires greatness in the reader. Each chapter challenges you take a deeper look at your life to bring out the person God has called you to be!... This book will change your life!"

- Terrence E. Trimuel

"Teen-Train has helped our daughter Hope and countless other young people to focus and express their visions that God has blessed them with. Through a myriad of events and programs--ranging from team training, career exploration, S.T.E.M. study, corporate field trips, interaction with professional speakers in the form of athletes to entertainers —Teen-Train has helped these young ambassadors to grasp and hone something that is as valuable as education itself--vision.

- Cynthia Sipp

THE PROCESS EQUALS THE PRODUCT
FORWARD PROGRESS ONE STEP AT A TIME

T. DWAYNE SMITH, SR., M.A., CLC

The Process Equals the Product:
Forward Progress One Step at a Time
Second Print Edition
ISBN 13: 978-0-9908109-0-2
Copyright © 2016, T. Dwayne Smith, Sr., M.A., CLC

Unless otherwise indicated, all Scripture quotations are taken from the King James Version of the Bible. Scriptures noted AMP are taken from the Amplified® Bible, Copyright © 1954, 1958, 1962, 1964, 1965, 1987 by The Lockman Foundation Used by permission. Scriptures noted NIV are taken from the HOLY BIBLE: NEW INTERNATIONAL VERSION®. Copyright © 1973, 1978, 1984 by International Bible Society. Used by permission of Zondervan Publishing House. All rights reserved. Scriptures noted GNT are taken from the Good News Translation® (Today's English Version, Second Edition) Copyright © 1992 American Bible Society. All rights reserved. Use by permission.

All photographs are open source distributed under a CC-BY 2.0 license.

Printed in the United States of America.
All rights reserved under International Copyright Law. Contents and / or cover may not be reproduced in whole or in part in any form without the express written consent of the author.

Team Unstoppable, Inc.
444 E. Roosevelt, Rd., Suite #254, Lombard, IL 60148
708.218.1104

TheProcessEqualsTheProduct.com
Feedback@ TheProcessEqualsTheProduct.com

contents

Dedications -- i
Acknowledgements -- iii
Special Thank You --------------------------------------- v
Foreword -- ix
Introduction --- xiii

Chapter 1 – The Process --------------------------------- 1

Chapter 2 – The Enemy of Excellence is Average 55

Chapter 3 – The Distorted Image ---------------------- 75

Chapter 4 – Attitude Determines Altitude ------------ 91

Chapter 5 – Finish the Work --------------------------- 113

Chapter 6 – The Product -------------------------------- 131

Say Something! -- 136

Bio Sketches – Notable People in History --------- 139

Biography Index --- 199

About the Author -- 202

Dedication

To my Lord and Savior - Jesus Christ: thank you for your love, grace, mercy, and personal sacrifice for me!

Acknowledgements

To My Wife Tannita...

You are so awesome and I love you dearly. I thank God for your strength, love, support, wisdom and prayers. You are my Best Buddy!

To My Children, Tarvies (TJ) & Timothy Smith...

The Bible says, *"A man's gift will make room for him and bring him before great men."* TJ and Tim, I pray that God will reveal your gifts to you, which will make your names great and bring you before great men. If you can dream it, you can achieve it. **Never stop dreaming and never let anybody put limits on you!** If your Daddy can do it with all the personal challenges I had to overcome as a young man, YOU CAN DO EVEN BETTER! Always remember, "You can do all things through Christ, who strengthens you." TJ and Tim, God is with YOU!

Love,
Dad

To Mom and Dad...

Thank you both for staying together and fulfilling your covenant vows, "To death do you part." Your commitment to each other has been our family's greatest example. Your marriage legacy is summed up in three words; "Pray, Say, and Stay!" Thank you for your example.

Love,
Dwayne

Additional Acknowledgements...

I want to acknowledge all the individuals too numerous to number, who have given me advice, feedback, direction, and shown me love through the process of getting this book written and published.

Special Thank You

Mr. Coleman, J. Sterling Morton Middle School Teacher

I want to thank you from the bottom of my heart. Meeting you in Middle School was divinely orchestrated by God Himself. My encounter with you was timely and God-ordained. You would not allow me to fail or accept failure as an option. You placed a demand on my potential and would not allow me to give anything less than my best!

Mr. Coleman, I will never forget how much you cared about each and every student in your classroom. You met us where we were and you facilitated an environment that allowed each student to experience personal success.

After I realized your impact on my life, I have been on a quest to positively impact every person—young and old—with the same simple formula: love, acceptance, support, consistency, and accountability! I don't know where you are today. However, I know for a fact that every person you have come into contact with has a better life as a result of you.

If I never see you again, I just want you to know that I appreciate you. You are an example of that ole saying, "it takes a village to raise a child." You were a leader in my village and I thank God for placing a Strong, Positive, Black, Male-Man in my life at that critical and crucial developmental stage of my life. I was going through a lot with the loss of my mother and the ongoing struggles of being young, black, and male on the Westside of Chicago.

You were the Moses sent to bring deliverance to me. I want to take this moment to say, "Thank You" for accepting the teaching assignment at J. Sterling Morton Middle School on Chicago's Westside. Your decision to work at Morton was the difference-maker in my life.

To Aunt Malinda & Uncle Frank...

Thank you for being there for me during some very difficult times in my life. You and Uncle Frank were very instrumental in my growth and development at a very critical time in my life. You opened up your home and your hearts and called me son! You provided food, clothing, support, guidance, and shelter to a young man who was angry, confused, and hurt. You held me accountable as a student and person of integrity to give nothing less than my very best. As a result of your diligence and commitment to my personal and academic success; I not only graduated on time, I graduated in the top 5% of my senior class! You taught me manhood; personal responsibility, hard work, endurance, and commitment! I am who I am today as a result of these life skills you taught me. Thank you!

You have been there for me and all my siblings. I'm forever grateful for your cooking, love, protection, direction, and example of personal sacrifice. Even though Uncle Frank has gone on to be with the Lord, Aunt Malinda you are not alone. You are loved and appreciated! Thank you for being there for me, John, Dee, and Jeanine. I pray that God will continue to keep you healthy, wealthy, and wise. Enjoy your retirement. YOU deserve it!

I Love You!

Dwayne

Foreword

Every now and then a book will just come along and catch you attention. The kind of book that makes you stop and take a closer look. Well, that is exactly the experience I had when picking up this book, *The Process Equals the Product*. Usually, when I read a book, I'll skim it or speed-read through so I can glean the major points and then, if necessary, I will go back and re-read it for retention. That did not happen with *The Process Equals the Product.*

Dwayne had me hooked from the very first chapter as he movingly recounts the annals of his childhood, explaining in vibrant detail the importance of environment, self-image, and the power of words. The very book itself seemingly radiates the energy of the author. Through witty and relevant examples, stories, and numerous real-life encounters—Mr. Smith takes the reader on a fast-paced, but meaningful look into their own lives, examining the choices they are making and the goals they are consciously or unconsciously setting. By the end of the book your arsenal will be filled with tools to shape your future into the destiny God has destined for you.

The wisest man who ever lived once penned these words:

"The purposes of a person's heart are deep waters, but one who has insight draws them out."

- Proverbs 20:5 NIV

Your special purpose is on the inside, laying dormant, until you draw it out. Other translations substitute the word "insight" for "wisdom." If you are wise, you will take the time to draw out your life's purpose through reading this book.

The book that you hold in your hands right now is a perfect example of how going through the process is not just what makes the product, but it is the product. No matter what age you are or what you have gone through—if you are a teen or an adult—reading this book is one of the best investments I believe you can make toward your present situation and future success.

If you are done settling for the good and are ready to move out onto the ledge of "best," this book is what you have been waiting for. Turn the page and experience the power of *The Process Equals the Product* for yourself!

Nathaniel Spiers
NathanielSpiers.com

Introduction

If You Don't Make The Choice, The Choice Will Make You!

Life is full of surprises; some good, some bad. What I have come to understand through my personal experiences is that life, essentially, is choice driven! God in His infinite wisdom has made provisions for each and every person to experience an abundantly good life. However, when disappointments, obstacles, challenges, and rejection knock at your door...

What will you do?

- Do you choose to quit, or will you choose to keep going?

- Do you choose to throw in the towel, or will you answer the bell for one more round?

- Do you choose to complain to God and others about how bad your situation has become, or will you choose to declare God's promises regarding the victory He has already promised you in His Word?

- Do you choose to settle for what you have, or will you choose to create what you want?

- Do you choose to focus on the problem, or will you readjust your lens (your thought process regarding the situation), and see the problem as an opportunity to grow and become a better person?

 These are choices and decisions that no one else can make except you!

As a youngster, I was told "if life gives you lemons, add some sugar and water to make lemonade!" During my teenage and young adult years, I was told that "success and failure share the same mindset—commitment." The central theme in both cases is that the choice is clearly yours to make. God, the creator of heaven and earth has given specific directions and instructions in His Word that

"Choose my instructions instead of silver, knowledge rather than choice gold..."
- Proverbs 8:10 NIV

"I call heaven and earth to witness this day against you that I have set before you life and death, the blessings and the curses; therefore choose life that you and your descendants may live."
- Deuteronomy 30:19 AMP

"If you will only obey me, you will eat the good things the land produces."
- Isaiah 1:19 GNT

You Have the Power to Choose!

In life, you will make mistakes and bad decisions. In some cases, people just continue in this vicious cycle of repeating the same mistakes and making bad decisions over, and over again. The point I want to impress upon you is that you have the power to make a choice and create the future you want for your life. My hope for everyone that reads this book is that you will slow down; consider the cost, pray, seek God's instructions, and then obey God. Your life is special and your time is valuable. Therefore, when you make a decision, put forth your best effort. Work hard and walk in integrity. Seize every opportunity to grow and learn as an individual. I like the quote President Abraham Lincoln said, "The best way to predict the future is to create it." You have the power and the ability to create the life you want!

I once heard someone say, "Life is a cruel teacher. She will give you the test first, then the answers." In my opinion, this is the worst way to learn because the end result could be too expensive. I highly recommend that you take a contrary approach to the mindset that "experience will be your teacher," and become proactive, intentional, strategic, and passionate about your future goals; aspirations, choices, personal and professional relationships. Don't be afraid to make mistakes because mistakes are a part of the learning process. Mistakes can help you grow and mature if you will learn from the experience. The only person I know who was perfect and never made a mistake was Jesus Christ. Everyone else in the Bible and in the history of mankind has made mistakes along the journey to achieve personal, relational, and financial success.

What is Success?

In my opinion, success is a personal journey and experience along the way to fulfill your dreams and aspirations in life. Along the journey to succeed, you will have to overcome may challenges and adversities. President Lincoln said it this way, "success is going from failure to failure without losing your enthusiasm." I love this quote because it says in essence that you are successful as long as you never give up or quit. Success is personal! We all have dreams, goals, and aspirations. We all have the power and ability to create the life we want no matter what race, gender, or age. You have the power.

In my own personal life, I have discovered that the secret to success is that there are NO short cuts, quick routes, or cookie-cutter templates. Like the great leaders before you and I, we have to make a choice, then a commitment. Martin Luther King, Jr., Nelson Mandela, and Gandhi all had to choose to be "leaders" and accept the great responsibilities that came along with the choice, even if it meant death! Your pedigree for SUCCESS is on the inside. It is your responsibility to work it from the inside-out.

chapter one

The Process

"You are special, unique and you will make a positive contribution to this world!"

Mr. Coleman, Teacher
J. Sterling Morton Middle School, Chicago, IL

Process is defined as continued forward development; progression; a method, and or procedure.

When I think of the word *process*, another word immediately comes to mind—*product*. I am sure that most of you have heard the following statements...

- "For every action there is an equal but opposite reaction."
- "For every start there is a finish."
- "To everything there is a season."

- "What you sow, you will reap."

And finally my quote: **"The process equals the product!"** The quotes can go on and on and on. The point I want to make is this, "nothing just happens!" Everything is a process.

Everything in life operates by way of a process. The **process** you sow determines the **product** you will reap. The earth was created by way of a process. A child developing inside a mother's womb is a process. If you had a master chef prepare an original dish one hundred times, that chef would use the same process every time to arrive at the same desired result or product. The chef uses the same step-by-step process to ensure that the product would successfully manifest time after time, after time...

Your personal relationship with God and your understanding of the Bible is a process. The product of that relationship is the direct result of you trusting the promises that are written in the Bible and walking in faith. Preparing for your future is a process. The product will be the end result of that preparation. If your product is undesirable, modify your process. **It's that simple!**

I was at a business conference some years ago. I heard one of the speakers make this simple, yet profound statement: **"if you want something different you have to be willing to do something different."** In other words, you will not experience change, until "You" make the change. You have to be willing to change your process in order to experience a different product or end result.

I would like to share part of my life process with you. My hope is that my personal experiences will ignite something inside you that will compel you to do something different in order to experience something different. The process is continual and subject to change with or without your approval and oftentimes without notification.

The Journey Begins!
April 1, 1979

As a young boy, I remember having this horrible dream that seemed so real. I could literally feel the tears streaming down the side of my face as I was asleep, or so I thought. All of a sudden, I hear two voices calling my name, "Dwayne, get up!" "Get up Dwayne!" "Dwayne, get up!" I quickly realized that the voices were my grandmother and aunt attempting to awake my brother John and I to inform us that our mother had transitioned from life to death while in the hospital.

I was between a state of sleep and consciousness and thinking to myself, "Am I dreaming or is this now my reality? Oh God, let it be anything but true!" I soon realized that my worst nightmare was now my devastating reality. As my grandmother and aunt shared the nature of my mother's death, my brother and I wept and embraced each other. The sadness was so overwhelming and the pain of the loss was so deep that I wanted to be with my mother in death at that very moment.

The mere thought of living life without my mother was unbearable. My father soon arrived with my sisters, Delores and Jeanine. We were all deeply saddened by the sudden loss of our beloved mother. I remember my mother having to go in and out of the hospital battling with various sicknesses and challenges in her body for the past two or three years. However, the thought never crossed my mind that she would check in the hospital and never check out again. I looked to my mom for strength, hope, joy, confidence, and faith in God. After all, she was my example. Now, who would fill her shoes and how can I make it without her? In my eyes, my mother was everything! However, I had to learn at a tender young age that this was only a part of my process of becoming the man I am today.

As I traveled home from my grandmother's house, I remained in disbelief. My state of mind was one of complete denial! It was unbelievable how my life had changed overnight. This was no April Fool's joke, even though my mother died on April 1st. I began to ponder the following questions: "How are we going to make it as a family?" "Why did my mother have to die?" "What am I going to do without my mother?" Questions even adults ponder after the loss of a close loved one.

While the grief cycle was taking its course, I became overwhelmed all at once. I was confused; full of fear, frustration, disbelief, and hopelessness. Life without my mother was something I could not or would not imagine. Can you fathom being a child, growing up motherless? Well, this was my situation and this process was not an easy one. To be honest, I had no indication that God would use this terrible circumstance and begin to build my trust, love, and understanding of Him as my source and provider. The Bible says, "What the enemy meant for evil, God will turn for our good."

Coping

After arriving home, my father did everything in his power to establish some sense of normalcy for the family. Dad spoke encouraging and supportive words that brought a level of relief knowing that mother was in a better place and her days of suffering were finally over.

As my father spoke these words of assurance to his children, I could see that he was not coping well with the loss of his beloved wife. I witnessed my father's motivation, desire, and will to live diminish with each passing day. My father was what you would call a "functioning alcoholic". After the death of my mother, his drinking progressively worsened to the point that his daily functionality became impaired. We would plead with our father to stop drinking. However, his response was always the same; "I'm grown," or "I know what I'm doing," and finally, "stay in a child's place!"... So, we did.

At that time I did not realize it, but now I understand that my father was experiencing extreme difficulties coping with the death of his wife, handling his emotions, and raising four children as a single male parent.

My dad was raised in a household where "real" men did not express their emotions. Being emotional in my father's mind was seen as a sign of weakness. In fact, I can't recall a time that my Dad openly cried or displayed any emotion until the death of my mother.

Hope Deferred

I hoped and prayed that God would help my father turn his life around, but it seemed like nothing was getting better, only worse. The passing of my mother triggered a downward spiral in my father's life and there was nothing we could do, but watch. In retrospect, the lesson is that you can pray, but faith without works is dead.

There must be corresponding action

Dad eventually became careless with his parental responsibilities. If it had not been for my older brother John stepping up and holding us accountable for respecting ourselves and honoring our curfew times, only God knows the disaster we could have faced as children. Thank you Lord for protecting us!

Eventually, our neighbors and extended family members became concerned about our safety, and someone anonymously notified the Department of Children and Family Services (DCFS). With all of the confusion and dysfunction that arose out of the DCFS involvement, somehow, someway, God made a way for us to remain together as a family. This battle was won, but the war was far from over! As time went on, I became increasingly bitter and angry with my situation. It wasn't long before I began to focus my anger and disappointment towards God, my Dad, and anybody else who did not understand what I was going through. It wasn't long before my motivation dissipated, along with my self-esteem.

After the passing of my mother, everything seemed so difficult and challenging. My dreams of becoming a doctor, lawyer, businessman, husband, and father were no longer a priority. Every account of my life's circumstance that I have relayed until now indicates that I was becoming a product of my environment. My environment became one of turbulence, uncertainty, fear, and frustration. Many youth and families in today's society can identify with these feelings. My environmental conditions were shaping my attitude, outlook, mindset, and finally, my behavior.

Environmental Conditions Influence Behavior

Believe it, or not!

Environmental conditions influence behavior. As a kid growing up, my environment has always impacted my behaviors, good or bad. The best illustration I have heard that demonstrates the influence that environment has on behavior is the story about the piranha and the goldfish.

Someone told me about an experiment where a Piranha was placed in a tank with a goldfish to prove the theory that environmental factors influence behavior. It doesn't take a rocket scientist to figure out that if you place a goldfish in the same tank with a piranha, the piranha will simply eat the goldfish.

However, a glass plate was inserted in the tank to create a divide between the goldfish and the piranha. What do you think happened? Initially, the hungry piranha went on an aggressive attack hitting his head up against the glass window trying to get to the goldfish. The frequency of the piranha's attempts to get the fish decreased day by day. After a week or so, the piranha became extremely passive and withdrawn. Finally, the glass was removed and the goldfish started to freely swimming around the tank and even brushing up against the now dying piranha.

The piranha soon died from starvation because he now had a mental block that told him he could not have access to the goldfish, so why even try?! The experiment proved that once the environmental conditions are set; attitudes, mindsets, and behaviors are now subject to the environmental conditions. The piranha went from having the potential and ability to pursue and devour its prey, to a mindset of despondency and hopelessness. How many people do you know have a mindset that they can't have the better things that life has to offer? They now think like the piranha, I can see it but I can't have it!

They have all the potential and ability yet, like that glass window that was placed in the tank to prevent the piranha from getting to the goldfish, satan has set up mental walls; barriers, and obstacles through environmental conditions that foster and reinforce a mindset of hopelessness, defeat, and despair. I can't, so why try?

Like the programmed mind of the piranha, you can see and hear about all the resources that are available to help you pursue your hopes and dreams. However, everything in your environment is saying, "you are not good enough," "you can't do it," "you don't have the skills," "no one else has done it before," and "why try, it will not work!" You dream of greatness, but your environment does not support, nor embrace your dreams. Usually, the end result is the same:

1. Starvation
2. Stagnation
3. Death

What do you think would have happened if Steve Jobs, Michael Jordan, Oprah Winfrey, Spike Lee, Tyler Perry, Bill Gates, Dr. Charles Drew, Fredrick Douglass, Martin Luther King, Jr., Booker T. Washington, George Washington Carver, or Dr. Bill Winston would have allowed the glass walls of their environments to stop them from pursuing their dreams? You don't have to answer, I will simply tell you. We would not know their story! We would not know their names! They would not be a part of American history for their accomplishments because they would not have stepped beyond the walls of containment to pursue their destiny!

> Environment sets the Atmosphere for potential to come forth

Environment is so important because it sets the atmosphere for your potential to come forth. The Piranha had the potential to pursue, overtake and devour the Goldfish. However, the environmental conditions that were set by the glass window restricted the Piranha's potential and reinforced a mindset of self-containment and limitation.

What is in your environment that is stifling, containing, and limiting your potential?

- Is it fear?
- Is it shame?
- Is it your last failure?
- Is it your last success?
- Is it lack of faith?
- Is it lack of motivation?
- Is it negative influences?
- Is it lack of knowledge?
- Is it YOU?

If God gives you a dream, TRUST God like Joseph did in the Bible and God will place you in the perfect situation so that your dream will become your reality. God knows the value and importance of the right environment. Sometimes the right environment is not the most comfortable place.

However, it's ideal for cultivating your gift and working your potential from the inside-out. God knows the impact of environment as it pertains to maximizing your potential and fulfilling your assignment. Satan is also aware of the importance and impact of environment. The devil understands that if he can keep you contained and in the wrong environment, your potential and creative ability becomes stifled; frustration starts to build, forward progress is compromised, and you inevitably forfeit your assignment and not fulfill your purpose for life.

However, I want you to know that God, who has begun a good work in you is faithful to complete it! God is so committed to your success that if your current environmental conditions are counterproductive to His will for your life, God will intervene and use friends, family members, circumstances and situations to move you into an environment that will place a demand on your full potential so you can come fulfill your assignment. Take, for example, the story of Joseph (Genesis Chapters 37 - 45). God gave Joseph a dream that would combat the global economic crisis that was forthcoming. When Joseph shared his awesome dreams of ruling and reigning as a king, his family did not embrace his dream. In fact, they despised him for sharing his dreams. After hearing Joseph's dreams, his family thought Joseph had a superiority complex over them and they despised him even more. Joseph's environment became one of tension, stress, turmoil, and sorrow...all the "right" elements to kill a dream! However, God intervened on Joseph's behalf and placed Joseph in the right environment where the gift would be embraced, encouraged, and sought-after until Joseph became what he dreamed: a ruler, a leader, and the answer for the world crisis in his time. Joseph's dream eventually became his reality.

Don't let your environment kill your dreams! Unlike that piranha, you don't have to die with your potential locked inside. Just like a seed requires the proper light, soil, and moisture to grow into a flower, God knows exactly what you need to grow into the success He ordained you to become even before the foundation of the world. You can trust that God will put you in the right environment to live out your full potential because God is a God of purpose and His will is for you and I to live a purpose–driven life.

Sticks and Stones...

Remember the age old adage: **"Sticks and stones may break my bones but words will never hurt me!"**

If you were told all your life: "you will never amount to anything," "you are not good enough," or "you are of no value or worth to anybody or anything," how do you think these negative deposits will impact your self-image and decision making? (Think about it!)

If you allow these negative words to linger and swim around in your mind, the effects of these words will eventually set up boundaries in your heart and potentially shift you away from the original plan God has for your life. The Bible says in Proverbs 23:7, **"For as he thinks in his heart, so is he."** This is a very powerful truth because it implies that if you can think and believe a certain way about yourself in your heart (yes, you can THINK with your heart...) it will be powerful enough to govern your attitudes, speech, relationships and ultimately, your actions and destiny in life.

Let's look at it from a positive perspective. If a person is told "you are smart," "you are a winner," "you make a difference," "if you can dream it, you can achieve it," the same spiritual law in Proverbs 23:7 goes into action. The force of these words will eventually build an image of success and confidence in your heart, and success will be your destiny. So, I would like to say it this way, "sticks and stones may break your bones, but words will determine your future!" What goes in, must come out! It's a law!

What Goes in Must Come Out!

When I was a kid, negative words were spoken to me, about me and over me. My actions were consistent with the words that were spoken about my life: negative attitude, mindset, behavior, and effort. My environment was one that fostered negativity, fear and defeat. If you poured coffee out of a pot and into a cup, the contents didn't change. The color, flavor, and temperature remains the same. Just because you took the coffee from one location to another didn't change the fact that what was in the pot is the same thing in the cup, coffee. The same concept holds true if your environment is one that fosters fear, unbelief, doubt, and negativity. The people that come from this type of environment will move on physically and relationally, etc. However, just like the coffee that was once in the pot and was poured into a cup; your attitude, mindset, and behaviors will reflect your environment. If you come from this type of dysfunctional environment, you may experience lack of confidence, low self-esteem, lack of respect for yourself and others, trust issues, pessimistic outlook on life, difficulties building and maintaining healthy relationships.

Now, Imagine a person with a distorted mindset like this teaching, training, mentoring and influencing the next generation of fathers, mothers, pastors, government elected officials, businessmen/women, and other leaders. We would have a vicious cycle of hurting people who are hurting other people!

No matter how you choose to articulate the concept, it all boils down to the same well known fact: "garbage in = garbage out!" Every seed must and will produce after its own kind! It's a law!

Words can produce both what you want and what you don't want!

Have you ever heard of a middle-school dropout? As a pre-teen, this was my aspiration. You may say, "Dwayne, you were just a kid, it was not that bad!" However, until you have walked a mile or better yet, a few steps in someone else's shoes, you can't fathom or understand the depth of emotional scarring that has taken place as a result of their life's experiences. At an early age, I witnessed the impact of negative words. My father did not desire anything for himself beyond the negative words that were spoken over him. My aunts and uncles did not desire anything beyond the words spoken over them. It had become a vicious cycle, a pattern of thinking, a way of talking, and a way of life... POISON!

Failure and Success Require the Same Amount of Energy

The same effort and energy that is required to achieve is required to underachieve. As a middle-school student, my test scores were poor and my attendance was terrible. I had an "I don't care" attitude and it required a lot of effort and energy to maintain my position. My behavior was an outward expression of internal hurt and pain that kept brewing with each passing day. When adversity and difficult situations came, we would support each other. However, we did not understand the depth of emotional hurt, pain, and trauma of each situation and its impact. After the death of our parents, we never received professional help to deal with our grief and the various cycles that take place when your are grieving.

Our support systems did not understand how to guide and facilitate healthy outlets that would help us with the healing process and acquiring emotional stability. I did what any pre-teen would do without mentoring, understanding and guidance. I adopted the "I don't care" attitude, suppressed my hurt and expressed my anger.

All It Takes Is One!

Mr. Coleman, my 8th grade teacher took a special interest in me and was concerned about my social and emotional development as a young man. Mr. Coleman challenged my thinking, attitude, behaviors and work output. Mr. Coleman's educational philosophy was simple, "give me your best and nothing but your best!" It was pretty obvious to Mr. Coleman that I was not giving my best effort; therefore Mr. Coleman continued to push, pull, and draw out my potential until he was convinced that I gave my absolute best. Mr. Coleman made a lasting impression on my life. In retrospect, I understand that Mr. Coleman recognized my state of mind and he slowly moved me out of a mindset of self-defeat, despair and failure into a mindset of confidence, personal accountability, and success. Mr. Coleman helped me to understand my potential and gave me the confidence to release that potential not only in the classroom, but in life. Mr. Coleman's efforts sparked passion, purpose, desire, and a thirst for success within me.

Mr. Coleman created a classroom environment that was both safe and conducive to learning. His daily message to his classroom was this, "You are special, unique and you will make a positive contribution to this world!"

To every teacher and parent who reads my book, please grasp this concept and run with it. Your children or students can learn and achieve success. Every person is born with purpose and potential. Embrace your children / students; take time to listen to them, spend time with them, make the things that interest them important to you, validate their feelings, love them, encourage them, and hold them accountable.

Demand Their Very Best and Nothing Less!

Your children / students will rise to the standard you set for them, whether low or high. I speak from personal experience that once Mr. Coleman placed a demand on my potential and he remained consistent with his expectations, I rose to the expectations he set for me. Until Mr. Coleman, no one demanded anything more from me than what I was already doing. Therefore, I had no standard to strive for beyond what I already experienced in life. The only expectation you should have for your children/students is SUCCESS! **Always remember that success is personal!** As a professional school counselor, mental health counselor, and life coach, I have three basic expectations for myself and the people I serve:

1. Take personal accountability for your choices and your actions.

2. Consistency is key: remain consistent in your efforts to improve and accomplish your goals.

3. Expected growth and embrace change.

You have to set the atmosphere for your children, students or employees to succeed. Mr. Coleman held me accountable, he was consistent with his expectations, and he established a structured learning environment that was conducive to success and achievement and as a result there was personal growth and I embraced the change process.

A Change for the Better

As a result of Mr. Coleman's positive attitude; affirming words, high academic expectations, and the win-win culture he established with his students, I personally began to believe in myself. My attitude changed, self-efficacy improved, and I made the honor roll for the first time in my life. This was something totally new for me and I was starting to enjoy success and the work that was required to be successful.

Things were starting to take a turn for the better in my life. As a result of one person taking the time to show genuine concern and demanding next level effort for success, my life changed for the better. The fact that this one teacher saw the value and worth for his students to not only grow as students—but as people—motivated change that extended beyond the four walls of that classroom, school, and community. Mr. Coleman was creating life-long learners, future responsible parents, leaders and world changers.

Divine Intervention

Finally, I was motivated to do better academically and personally. I was now looking forward to high school and the new opportunities that were awaiting me. In the community where I grew up (Chicago's Westside), gang recruitment and gang violence was a major problem. Gangs were growing in size and the violence was becoming more and more fierce. Drugs, prostitution, and poverty were in and around my community. Out of concern for my safety and to avoid gang involvement, I would run to school and back home everyday and take alternate routes to avoid gang involvement, if possible. The area where I grew up (Fulton and Homan), the top two gangs were the Black Souls and Vice Lords. My safety concerns were always outside of school, but never in a million years did I think it would be an issue in school until the day I walked into a gang recruitment session. The gang held recruiting in the boys bathroom in my school, of all places—wrong place, wrong time!

All I remember was that the bathroom was completely filled with gang members and they were actively recruiting everyone that walked into that bathroom. You either had two choices; join now or get beat up and join later. THERE WAS NO WAY OUT and I was next in line. I was scared to death. It was total mayhem in that bathroom. Before I could react and attempt to run out of the bathroom, someone grabbed me and slammed me up against the wall. Immediately, the guys started to question my gang affiliation. I was petrified because at that moment I thought I was going to die! I didn't want to be in a gang because I knew what it meant and I knew the end result. I was in big trouble and I knew it at that very moment! I remember closing my eyes and saying these four simple words, "God, please help me!" That was all I knew to say at that moment.

Suddenly, a loud voice pierced through the noisy crowd, and I heard these three words, "Let Him Go!" "I said, let him go!" "He is not gang material!" Immediately, the guy who held me against the wall let me go and backed up off me. I opened my eyes and saw all the gang members backing down at the commands of whom I presumed to be their leader. The leader looked at me, grabbed me and shoved me out of the bathroom and told me to Go NOW! He didn't have to tell me twice because I ran so fast out of that bathroom and didn't stop until I was back in my classroom. Needless to say, I never went back into that bathroom again and I never walked the hallways alone after that incident.

Some weeks had passed since that potentially life threatening encounter and I began to ask around to see if anyone knew of the gentleman who intervened on my behalf because I wanted to personally thank him. To my surprise, nobody recognized him by description and I never saw him again. It was at that moment that I realized that those four words, "God, please help me" that I prayed in that bathroom was God answering my prayer: Divine Intervention.

My freshman year in high school, I had a similar encounter while walking home from school with one of my classmates. We were approached and surrounded by a local gang. This happened so suddenly that we did not have a chance to react. I felt the same feelings I felt in that bathroom. As the gang closed in, I remember closing my eyes (again) quickly and crying out, "God, help me!" All of a sudden, there was some confusion and my classmate took and ran off across the street leaving me alone and surrounded by the gang. Almost immediately after my classmate took off, the entire gang went after him. I was left untouched and standing all alone wondering what just happened? I could not believe with my eyes what I saw. It occurred so fast, but it seemed like it happened in slow motion. I looked in the eyes of the gang members. It was as if they couldn't see me... as if someone or something was shielding me from danger. Once again, I was reminded of the simple, yet powerful prayer that I prayed at that very moment, "God, help me!" God divinely intervened and I knew it. I'm reminded of God's saving grace and the account in the Bible (Matthew 14:29-31) when Peter walked on the water and go to Jesus. When he saw the winds, fear gripped him and he began to sink. The Bible says that Peter cried out three simple words, "Lord, save me" and immediately Jesus reached out his hand and caught Peter. Like Peter, I needed help and God intervened. From that moment forward, I never had another problem with gangs. Thank you Jesus! God will give you the desires of your heart and it was not my desire to be a gang member and God honored my desire. **I was NOT gang material!**

Leaving the Past Behind

We were moving forward as a family. My dad surprised us all and purchased a new home outside of the negative influences of our old community. The move could not have come at a better time, because the area that we lived in was now heavily drug and gang infested.

We were so proud and happy about the decision our father made to move our family. The future was looking better and brighter. I went from a kid who wanted to drop out of middle school to now, a freshman at John Marshall Metro High School.

I began to acknowledge and recognize God's presence in my life. Doors were starting to fly open and it seemed as if people were "on assignment" to encourage me. My immediate family was very supportive and I began to acquire positive friendships with people like my life-long friends Obrien Jenkins, Eric Walker, and Derrick Jones. I had wonderful teachers who continued to challenge me and place a demand on my potential. My freshman division teacher made a profound statement when she said these words the first day of school, "this is the start of a new beginning!"

The Bible tells us, in Proverbs 18:21, **"Death and life are in the power of the tongue; and they that love it shall eat the fruit thereof."**

Words Have Power

All the talk about success finally convinced me that I could be successful. This was unfamiliar territory for me. There had been a time not so long ago when all I had thought about was failing. I was scared, nervous, and didn't know what to expect. However, what I did know (or was beginning to discover) was that LIFE IS CHOICE DRIVEN – and I decided to be successful no matter what!

Your Life is the Sum Product of Your Choices!

I had come to the realization that I could not control what others around me were doing.

However, I could control how I responded to the different situations and circumstances that may come my way in life. It did not matter anymore that my mother was deceased. The fact that my father was a functioning alcoholic has no impact on my decision to remain positive. The dysfunctional dynamics of my home-life was no longer a factor to me. What other people thought about me did not matter anymore. I finally realized that I had the resources, power, and ability to choose my future. Sometimes the different obstacles, potholes, and challenges are out of your control and not a byproduct of your own doing. However, your attitude and response in dealing with the various circumstances and situations becomes your sole responsibility.

You also have the power and ability to choose where you end up in life. So, I challenge you to stop making excuses. Stop saying, "They" made you do it! Nobody can make you do anything. You can make up your mind today to be successful even if you just failed a class, got fired from a job, have sickness in your body, went through a divorce, or lost a loved one—you have the power

to choose your response.
Choose Y-o-u-r D-e-s-t-i-n-y!

All in the Master's Plan

My father continued to encourage me to work hard and to do my very best in school. He was excited because I was finally bringing home respectable grades that made him proud. After my freshman year in high school, I received my first job through a summer employment program where I was tutoring middle school aged students. Before, I didn't even care about my own life or education plans. Now, I'm inspiring and assisting others to work hard and to stay focused on their academic goals and future aspirations in school.

The Bible says in **Jeremiah 29:11 AMP, "For I know the thoughts and plans that I have for you, says the Lord, thoughts and plans for welfare and peace and not for evil, to give you hope in your final outcome."**

God has a GOOD plan for everyone! All we have to have is faith in what God said in His Word!

I was really feeling good about the success I was experiencing in my life. It did wonders for my self-esteem and confidence. I had a successful freshman year of high school and my first paying job. I often think about the Bible story of David and Goliath. David had to overcome many challenges, such as slaying a lion and a bear before he had the confidence to take on the ultimate challenge—the giant, Goliath! Like David, you and I must come face to face with obstacles and challenges so that we can build character, confidence, and faith. No matter what obstacles we face as we travel this road called DESTINY, God is with us and His Plan for us is GOOD!

Daddy, I Need You!

After completing my freshman year of high school, I obtained my first paid summer job. This was an exciting time because I had an opportunity to earn $540 dollars for the summer and it was much needed at the time. While working my summer job, my relation with my father began to take a turn for the worst because my father wanted me to give him my extra money instead of using it to purchase my school supplies, clothing, etc. My dad asked me to assume some of the financial duties around the house and it was cool at first because I wanted to help out and I appreciated the sacrifices that my father was making for his children. However, school was about to start soon and I needed clothing, supplies, and materials headed into my second year of high school. My father didn't seem to understand my position, so he gave me an ultimatum: pay bills in the house or get out! I didn't agree with my father's position and our differences of opinion caused friction and tension in our relationship. I remember one evening my father got angry and upset with me over money. He went into his bedroom and got his gun and told me to get out of his house. If I didn't leave he was going to blow my head off. I was scared and angry at the same time. I was a sophomore in high school; no income, and now homeless. I could not believe this was happening. I felt my dad was being unreasonable, unfair, and mean. It appeared as soon as things were coming together in my life, they were now quickly coming apart!

I asked my father if I could call my Aunt Malinda and Uncle Frank to see if they would come and pick me up. My dad yelled at the top of his voice, "I want you out of my house - you can go to the streets for all I care!" My Uncle came over and attempted to calm my dad down while I packed my things to leave. I was so hurt and I felt so rejected by my father. This was a very difficult time for me because I loved my dad; I didn't want to leave my family and this was my first time being away from my brothers and sisters.

I was overwhelmed with sadness because I knew my father was challenged with his health from the accumulation of excessive cigarette smoking; drinking alcohol, stress, and poor eating habits.

Total Recall

May 30, 1984

My father passed away from a massive heart attack. My dad was only 42 years old.

I can recall the day my father died. On May 30, 1984, my Uncle Frank received an emergency phone call from a mutual friend regarding my father's health. My uncle and I immediately rushed to the aid of my father. During the ride, I began to reflect on my time with my father and my mother. The feelings of fear; anxiety, anger, and despair quickly began to consume me once again. My brother John and younger sister Jeanine were already present when I arrived. My older sister, Dee had just received the news and was on her way to meet us.

My father was sitting in the living room with a distressed look on his face. It was sad and painful to see him in this condition. I remember sitting at his feet encouraging him that everything was going to be fine even though I could see that dad was struggling to breathe. Once my sister Dee-Dee arrived, she began to comfort Jeanine, while John was trying to get things under control. I was scared because the situation did not look good at all. I remained at my fathers' feet, watching, waiting, listening, and hoping he would hold on until the ambulance arrived. My father, who never showed signs of weakness or emotion continued to assure us that he was ok and that he needed some air and a glass of water.

My father and I began to reconcile our differences and I asked for his forgiveness for what happened between us. I apologized for my actions and I told my father that I loved him. My father responded that he loved me and for me to forgive him for his actions. My father looked me in the eyes and told me everything was going to be fine.

I am proud and thankful to say without hesitation to all the readers of this book that my Dad was a praying man. I remember times when I, or one of my siblings, would have to wake my father up because he would have fallen asleep while on his knees praying. My father had confidence that God was going to take care of his children in the event that something happened to him.

The paramedics finally arrived and assisted my brother and uncle to get my dad out of the house and into the ambulance for immediate medical attention. While the paramedics were tending to dad, I found myself comforting my sisters as we all embraced and believed that everything was going to be ok. Daddy will pull through this and we were going to be ok as a family.

How Do I Say Goodbye – Again!

The paramedics continued their emergency procedure on my father for approximately 30 minutes before driving off to the hospital. In my heart, I knew it was a very bad situation and that my father may not make it. However, I kept telling my mind to calm down, stay in control, don't think negative thoughts—Dad is going to be alright! We immediately followed the ambulance to the hospital and once we arrived, our father was pronounced dead. I felt so empty and numb. I didn't know how to express what I was feeling because I didn't know how to feel at that moment.

The adjustment after the death of my father was difficult because he was the stabilizing force for the family after the death of our mother. The difference this time is that we had experienced death once before with the loss of our mother and we all knew at that moment that we, (my siblings and I) had to make it happen!

A Work In Progress

After the funeral and burial of my father, I made up my mind that I would not allow the legacy of my parents to go up in smoke! I was going to work harder, get focused and maintain a positive attitude. I had the opportunity to eat from two different tables, "the table of past failures and defeat" and now, "the table of current success and forward progress." It didn't take a rocket scientist to realize which table offered the better options: "the table of success.and forward progress" Therefore, I remained seated and continued to "eat success" regardless of my personal circumstances. I was determined that I was not going to give in to my emotions. I knew that in order for me to survive the proverbial "death blow", I had to reach beyond my limited understanding and look to God for guidance, strength, wisdom, understanding, peace and His Grace!

Pomp and Circumstance

High School Graduation:
John Marshall Metro High School.

This was a day long in coming! Not only did I graduate, but I graduated with high honors! I excelled academically, socially, and relationally. I remember sitting on the stage at my graduation among other distinguished members of the National Honor Society in our white gowns thinking and reflecting on the process and journey that led to the following results:

- Top five percent of my graduating class
- Membership in The National honor Society
- Who's Who Among American High School Students
- The Principal's Scholars Program
- The John Hope African American Club
- Recipient of the distinguished Chicago Mercantile Exchange Essay Contest Award, presented by the late Chicago Mayor Harold Washington
- Member of The All City Academic Olympic History Team 1st Place Winners
- Homecoming King
- Accepted into 18 different colleges and universities

All this went through my mind while I was sitting

on that stage with the top academic students of my graduating class. Although my parents were not physically present to share in this momentous occasion, I felt them with me in spirit. Especially, when I received my high school diploma, I imagined them looking down from their sky box in heaven saying, "That's my boy!" Mom and Dad, this diploma is for you!

The Transformation Continues...

I was college bound! I was excited! I made it out of the "hood!" Praise God!

The first day I arrived at Eastern Illinois University (EIU) I was nervous, but my Aunt Malinda was with me every step of the way as were my best friends Obrien Jenkins, Eric Walker and Derrick Jones. I thank God for friends, "The Westside Crew" because we held each other accountable, focused, and moving towards the ultimate goal – a college degree!

The four years I spent in college were filled with new and exciting experiences. I met a lot of people, attended social gatherings and was involved in a variety of campus activities. I joined Phi Beta Sigma Fraternity Inc., and enjoyed the national, community, and campus benefits of membership. The entire college experience was awesome, yet I still had this feeling that something was missing in my life.

Destiny is Calling...

In the summer of 1991, I was the first in my family to earn a four year degree. I successfully obtained my Bachelors of Arts (B.A.) Degree in Psychology. My plan after graduating was to return home, get a job and be reunited with my family. However, God had a different plan. I was introduced to a potential employment opportunity that would pay for me to obtain a Master's Degree, while gaining professional working experience as a Graduate Assistant with the EIU Housing Department. Returning to EIU was certainly not part of my original plan. However, I decided to interview for the position because I really didn't have any other concrete options at the time.

Even though I applied for the assistantship, I really didn't have any expectations beyond the application process because I didn't meet the minimal requirements for the position. After my graduation ceremony, I figured my time at EIU was finished. One of my best friends and fellow college graduate, Eric Walker, obtained a position in the child welfare industry back home in Chicago and he shared his connections with the hopes that I would obtain a position within the same agency. However, before anything could materialize, I received a phone call from Eastern's Housing Department offering me a graduate assistantship position with the opportunity to obtain my Master's Degree as part of my graduate package. I was taken by surprise because I was not mentally prepared to return back to school for another classroom experience. However, I was not gainfully employed and I really didn't have a plan of action regarding my next move in life. I felt a sense of peace and excitement about the offer so I accepted the graduate assistantship position.

During the long road trip back to campus, there was plenty of opportunity for doubt to seep in regarding my decision to return back to the EIU campus. I started to question myself... "Did I make the right choice?" I could hear the voices of my family and friends taunting me saying, "Dwayne is scared of the real world!"

Truthfully, I was scared but I could not figure out if the root of my fear was the fear of failure or the fear of success. You know, sometimes you think you are doing the right thing, but you really don't know if you are. That's when you have to be still and let peace speak. Sometimes you should question your decisions. I encourage you to pray and ask God to give you peace during your decision making process. When you are "at peace" about your decision(s), follow peace and not the voices of the people around you... I recommend that you employ the following four steps when making any decision—no matter how big or small:

1. Pray.
2. Remove yourself from people and their opinions.
3. Listen for God.
4. If you don't have peace, don't do it.

As I reflected on my decision to go back for the graduate assistantship and advanced degree, I had a sense of peace about my decision. In retrospect, I never took time to plan and prepare beyond college beyond my B.A.. The point that became crystal clear for me was a college degree without a career will put you on the path of frustration and the road to un-fulfillment. That old saying still stands true, if you fail to plan—you plan to fail.

New Process, New Product

Everything seemed to be going well in my new found direction in life. I was gaining professional work experience; building lasting relationships while, obtaining a Masters degree—debt free! What a blessing! I felt like I was in my purpose and it felt great! However, the thirst to fill the mysterious void continued to linger. I felt a sense of emptiness and I could not figure out why. Have you ever felt like you were helping others but nobody was helping you? I couldn't do enough busy work to quiet the emptiness that kept screaming out within me. I remember this one student who worked on staff with me in the housing department named Todd Rittenhouse. He had the stature of a professional football lineman, yet a gentle heart and soft spoken voice. It seemed like nothing ever upset Todd and he was consistently nice all the time. Todd and I became very close while working together and he would often talk about Jesus Christ and His message of hope, love, forgiveness, mercy, and grace. I will never forget when Todd spoke the following words that pierced my heart and rocked my world. Todd said to me,

"Dwayne, that void in your life – only Jesus Christ can fill it! No matter how nice you are or how much you help others, the emptiness that you are feeling, only Jesus Christ can take it away and replace it with His love. All you need to do is open up your heart and receive Him as Lord and Savior."

At that moment, I realized that Todd was right. However, like most people I did not receive Christ on the first call even though the words Todd spoke bore witness in my heart and I knew it was the truth! God wanted to show me how much He loved me and all I needed to do was allow Him to simply DO IT!

Immediately, after that encounter with Todd, it seemed like God began to strategically place other Christian brothers in my life; Ray McElroy, Jeff Rucker, and Terrence Trimuel all shared God's love and message of grace with me. These brothers would encourage me and often invite me to church. I always had excuses for every invitation. Over time, I began to feel a desire to attend because everything these brothers were sharing with me "ministered" peace and comfort to my soul and it bore witness with my spirit.

My Lord and Savior

I will never forget when I invited Jesus into my heart. It was Sunday, September 20, 1992, at EIU's University Baptist Church. The Pastor was preaching about God's love and the power of Jesus' death, burial and resurrection. After his message, he invited people to receive Jesus as their personal Lord and Savior. At that moment, I felt like the spot light was on me - God was speaking directly to me. I felt a strong pull and desire for God like never before. I asked Jesus to come into my heart and I repented of my sins.

Suddenly, an indescribable peace overcame me and all I could do was cry uncontrollably. It was the greatest feeling in the world—unspeakable joy! I felt the weight and pressures of the world lift off my shoulders. The shame of my childhood; growing up without parents, deep seeded hurt, rejection, loneliness, feelings of failure, and the anger I felt towards God after the death of my parents were all being loved away by Jesus Christ!

The thought that God loved me so much that He sent His Son to die for my sins, shortcomings, imperfections, and weaknesses brought overwhelming joy to my life. I realized that God loved me, accepted me and was now Father to me!

During the summer of 1993, I completed my M.A. and was offered a full time Hall Director position with Eastern's Housing Department. I took the job and I continued to develop my faith in God and my love-walk with people. I knew God was preparing me for the next level and I was ready and willing.

After completing my third year in the housing department, God opened a door of opportunity for me to return back home to Chicago with my family, friends, and a new church home. I started working in the child welfare industry serving disadvantaged, at-risk wards of the state. Everything God was teaching me about love and patience would be applied in my new career path to help youth and families from diverse backgrounds find their path of purpose and destiny.

Promotion Comes from God

After seven months, God shifted me into another department working specifically with teens in preparation for adulthood. God continued to bless me as He said He would in Ephesians 3:20,

> ***"...now unto him that is able to do exceeding abundantly above all that we ask or think, according to the power that worketh in us."***

I asked God to be a blessing to youth and He had gave me favor with those around me by promoting me to the Supervisor of Educational and Vocational Training and Resources. My responsibility was to impact the lives of youth through educational and vocational training, planning and placement. I was the kid who grew up without direction, hope, and parental guidance, yet God used my skills and personality to train youth and families to understand their purpose and to release their full potential.

A Continual Process

God continues to work in my life. Process is ongoing and we have to trust God and stay in faith. FEAR (False Evidence Appearing Real) has the capacity to come into our lives to stifle growth with the end result of stagnation. Repeat after me, **"No Fear Here!"** Say it again, **"No Fear Here!"**

The experiences that I've shared with you are testimonies designed to build confidence and faith in God. Do not be afraid of the process or the unknown! Do not be afraid of change and do not be afraid to take the journey alone.

Trust God!

The Bible says in Deuteronomy 20:4,

"For the Lord your God is going with you! He will fight for you against your enemies, and He will give you victory!"

As you are walking through this process we call "life," stay encouraged.

Self-Reflection/Life Application
Chapter 1: My Process

1. Take a moment and reflect on a personal challenge you may have had or may be currently experiencing. This challenge may be personal, academic, or relational. Describe this challenge in detail.

___

2. What has been your approach or attitude to overcome this challenge? Have you allowed the challenge to become a barrier to stop your forward progress?

___

3. The writer talks about the correlation between environmental factors and thinking/behavior. He utilized the illustration of the piranha and the goldfish. Share how the environmental factors in your life influence your thinking and behavior?

_____
_____
_____
_____
_____
_____
_____

4. Think about a personal challenge or struggle. Circle the word that best describes your outlook regarding your situation 9 out of 10 times?

OPTIMISTIC   PESSIMISTIC

5. Think about a personal success in your life. Share what made you most proud of that moment and why.

_____
_____
_____
_____

Please Note: There are more in-depth questions provided in the accompanying workbook that will enhance your learning/growing experience.

chapter two

The Enemy of Excellence is Average

"Average is half as good as the best, twice as good as the worst!"

John Avanzini
Evangelist

Average: Lacking any extraordinary, untypical, or exceptional characteristic; regular; ordinary; normal; common.

Excellent: Of a very high quality or standard; to exceed; to be exceptional; to outdo; to be very good; first rate; to be pre-eminent; worthy of choice.

There are over 7 billion people on the earth and not one person has the same eye retina, fingerprint or DNA spiral. No other person possesses your unique set of gifts, talents or abilities. Just as no two snowflakes are alike, you are like no one else on this entire earth. God created you with unlimited potential and God made it that NOBODY would have your "God-given potential!" In the words of my pastor, Dr. Bill Winston, "God has made you a specialist with no equal."

God, the Creator of Heaven and Earth uniquely designed you and gave you individuality that sets you apart from anybody else on the earth. You are an original! Think about it for a moment; God gave you special gifts and talents so that you would stand out as someone special. When you use your gifts and talents to serve others, God is glorified. Your unique expression of gifts and talents qualifies you to be in a class all by yourself without any competition. Your potential speaks to your destiny and the assignment you are to fulfill on the earth.

Nobody can operate in your unique individual calling or "assignment." This gift and ability that God has given you was uniquely crafted and designed for you and you alone. When God made you, He broke the mold, and that's why it is criminal for you to attempt to be someone else or for someone to attempt to be you. You are not a copycat. You are an original! Your gift was not given by an *average* God, but a God of *excellence*.

One day the Lord led me to do a word study on the words "average" and "excellence." While researching those words, I discovered that the word "average" is not mentioned nor is it used in the Bible even one time! However, the word "excellent" is recorded in the Bible a total of 65 times: 26 times in the Old Testament and 39 times in the New Testament. Not only is "excellent" mentioned, it was used as an adjective to describe the nature and characteristics of God.

> With Great Power, Comes Great Responsibility

This is pretty significant when you think about the fact that you and I have unique gifts, talents and abilities. Your nature and characteristics are directly related to your calling and assignment. The gift God has given you has everything to do with your calling and this is why YOUR enemy is "average-thinking."

Average-thinking people will put pressure on you to compromise the excellence that is within you. You will eventually adopt a mindset of normal, common, and ordinary thinking. These patterns will keep you in a place where you will no longer desire excellence or strive to set a high standard for others to strive for in their expression of their giftedness. When you operate in your area of gifting, you will not only get the attention of your peers, you will command the attention of the world! This is why the enemy of excellence is average! Average thinking people know that if you embrace your unique God-given talent and cultivate that talent through hard work, discipline and laser focus, you become UNSTOPPABLE!

This is why I love the words Uncle Ben spoke to Peter Parker in the movie, The Amazing Spiderman, "With great power, comes great responsibility!" What I believe Uncle Ben was trying to get Peter to see, was that he was special and his talents and abilities were not just for himself but in the service of others.

Greatness is on the inside of you and as you work out your potential, think of the words Uncle Ben spoke to Peter Parker, "with great power comes great responsibility." The world is waiting on you to discover your greatness and if you use your greatness to serve others, the entire world benefits. The Bible says that God formed you from the womb, (Isaiah 44:24). You were in the mind of God long before you came onto this earth. Therefore, your very existence speaks of your value; worth, and importance to God and the impact you make in the lives of your family, friends, community, school, and even the nation. God could have chosen anybody to be born any date and time in the history of this world. However, He saw fit for you to be born in this dispensation of time for a specific work and assignment that can ONLY be completed by you. YOU ARE SOMEONE SPECIAL!

The Bible says, in Romans 8:19 (AMP),

> ***"For (even the whole) creation (all nature) waits expectantly and longs earnestly for God's sons to be made known (waits for the revealing, the disclosing of their sonship)."***

This Scripture is clear in saying that people all over the world (young and old) are waiting on God's people to raise the standard of excellence. Thereby God's demonstrated grace, love, and power would command the attention of the world. God is a God of excellence and He wants to display His excellency through our gifts and completed assignments. When you and I accept the call or assignment that God has for our lives, God will then give specific instructions to successfully complete the assignment. When the assignment is fulfilled, God is glorified because people all over the world will be blessed as a result of your obedience to the call of excellence! Average thinking has cost this nation a lot of grief; loss, and economic hardship. Think about the overwhelming numbers of teen drop-outs, pregnancies, crime, and violence that continue to impact this nation. If people in general established a standard of excellence for themselves, others would begin to follow their example and work hard to fulfill their personal and professional goals.

If you do not fulfill the assignment you were born and purposed to do, that assignment may go undone or someone else may fulfill the assignment in a very different way that is not God's best. The reason why it would not be God's "best" is because you were created for that specific assignment and if you accepted the call, excellence would be the end result. If you settle for a life of average, people who admire you will follow your "average-compromising mentality" that will be perpetuated for generations. Instead of people striving to express their true God-Potential, we have people walking around unknowingly lacking any extraordinary, untypical, or exceptional characteristic or true unique expression of their abilities and God given talent.

Your individuality is a big deal to God! God created you to express His Glory on the earth through your unique gifting and individual talent. Remember what Uncle Ben told Peter Parker, "with great power comes great responsibility". You have a personal responsibility to utilize your gift to touch the lives of other people in a positive way. If you are willing and obedient, God can use your gift to help someone else strive for excellence, and share their unique gifting with others and the world.

God did not create anything average! Everything and every person was created extraordinary;

unique, different, and exceptional—an "original." Why did God create every person different? Why did God "break the mold" after creating each and every person uniquely differently than the next person? I believe God did this to express His creative ability and to set us all apart so that each individual person would have equal opportunities to share with the world their unique value and worth and God will get the glory.

Think about the definition of average and the definition of excellence. Average is regular, ordinary, normal, common. Whereas excellence is very high quality or standard; to exceed; to be exceptional; to outdo; to be very good; first rate; to be pre-eminent; worthy of choice.

Take for example, the 90's Championship Chicago Bulls. They were described as unbeatable, unstoppable, unbelievable, simply stated..."the best!" The Bulls, in my opinion, set a standard of excellence for all professional sports. They won a total of six World Championship Titles; (1991-93 and 1996-98). The Chicago Bulls were not an average basketball team. There is no way you can win three championships back to back for a total of six championships playing average basketball!

Their approach to the game, both on and off the court, was excellent. The level of professionalism, commitment to the team concept, mental and physical preparation, attitude, and personal sacrifice was nothing less than excellent! They were not satisfied with just being good or average. The Bulls wanted to be the best ever and they proved it during their 1996 season, setting a new record of 72 wins/10 losses, breaking the Los-Angeles Lakers' record of 69 – 13 that had been set in the early 1970s.

The Bulls established a model and template for success that can be applied both personally and professionally. It's called "hard-work, personal sacrifice, and team-work." The formula for success was very simple; go the extra mile, work harder, self-discipline, focus on your goals, personal sacrifice, and never settle for average—strive for excellent!

There is no reward for average, only for excellence!

Let's look at the word excellent. **Excellent** means to surpass; to exceed; to be exceptional; to outdo; to be very good; first rate; to be pre-eminent; worthy of choice.

When you look at the definition of excellent, you can see that God had something special on His mind when He thought of His ultimate creation, Mankind! God crafted the human-race out of Himself so that we would display His excellence and receive recognition and honor for our gifts and talents. Knowing that excellence is part of your genetic make-up, why would you settle for a lifestyle that is contrary to your genetic make-up or DNA?

This point reminds me of the story of the prodigal son. When he became of age he asked his father for his inheritance so he could pursue a lifestyle contrary to his birthright and genetic make-up. The Bible tells us that the prodigal son exhausted all of his resources and he was no longer the "life of the party." I can imagine the shame, disgrace, and embarrassment he must have felt when he was alone and had time to reflect about his decisions and his choices. Like so many people, the prodigal son compromised his value system, self-worth, and God-given potential. Instead of displaying his talents and walking in God's will for his life, the prodigal son became distracted with popular opinions, gaining acceptance from his peers, and being status-quo. The prodigal son made a decision to surround himself with "average" thinking people instead of "exceptional" thinking people. Exceptional thinking people are people who dream and think about space travel; entrepreneurship opportunities, pastoring the next mega church, writing books that change people for the good, coming up with the cures for life-threatening diseases, becoming the next Steve Jobs, Bill Gates, or Dr. Bill Winston.

The Bible says in Luke 15:17-18, the prodigal son came to his senses and decided to return home to his father's house where he was restored to his rightful place and was now back in the will of God for his life. This story reminds me that if we are not careful, we can get distracted to the degree that it can cost us our calling and assignment. Sometimes we think what God has for us is not good enough and we begin to seek acceptance in all the wrong places. Average-thinking people can't celebrate "exceptional" thinking people. when we allow God to shine in and through us, our gifts become like light that shines, exposes, and brings separation from "average" accomplishments or results. Unfortunately that old saying still holds true to this day, "birds of the same feather flock together and most times end up in the same place."

Average was not a word God used to describe any of His creation. Everything that was created was uniquely created. I heard someone say that there are over 8.7 million different types of living species on the earth and even more different ones are being discovered every day. It is utterly amazing to see God's creative ability and originality when you realize that He thought of every individual person and living species that exists in the earth. God placed the same creative abilities inside each and every person to create something so unique that the whole world would stop, look, marvel and admire your unique talents and abilities.

> Your Identity is Expressed through your Calling

Think about all the sculptures, paintings, songs, clothing, cars, books, houses, and electronic devices that exist today. What brings the value to each of these inventions and ideas is the fact that they are all uniquely different in one way or another.

When we attempt to act like someone else, we risk forfeiting our calling and birth-assignment. There is a tendency for children tend to emulate their parents attitudes and perspectives because through observation, association, and teaching that is ongoing and constantly reinforced either inside or outside the home. However, the assignment and call that God has placed on the inside is different from person to person. This is why we hear so many stories about kids who have famous parents and the kids are going in a totally different direction with their career aspirations.

At one time, everybody wanted to "Be like Mike!" When Michael Jordan played basketball in the NBA the whole world watched with amazement. He played the game effortlessly, naturally, and in a spirit of excellence that commanded the attention and respect of the entire world. Michael Jordan became a global icon and he is the primary reason that the NBA gets the world recognition that it receives today.

Michael Jordan retired from the game several times before his final and official retirement in 2003 from the Washington Wizards. The NBA is still looking for another Michael Jordan. Sure you have LeBron James and Kobe Bryant, but there will never be another Michael Jordan. Why? Because God only made one Michael Jeffrey Jordan.

Your calling speaks directly to your individuality. For example, identical twins share the same egg in the womb. However, each twin has a specific assignment that speaks directly to their interests, likes, and dislikes. They were conceived from the same egg yet, they are two completely different people with their own individual dreams, aspirations, and desires.

When you look throughout the Bible you will find that God called and appointed many different men and women for different assignments. Some were called to preach, teach, fight wars, or rebuild and restore nations. In all of these situations, the assignments spoke directly to the purpose for being born into the world and each and every person that completed their assignment left a mark that will never be erased.

How Excellent is Thy Name!

God is a God of excellence! Even His name is excellent in all the earth (Psalms 8:9). The spirit of excellence that God placed inside of you and I was purposed for identification, recognition and honor.

You may think that excellence is a very difficult standard to live up to or to achieve. However, the truth is that it takes just as much effort; focus, and commitment to operate from a mindset of average thinking as it would to operate from a mindset of exceptional thinking. The story and life of Daniel in Holy Bible is a great example of someone who embraced his gifts and talents and did not compromise the assignment. Daniel decided that he was going to be excellent and not average. As a result of his commitment, Daniel was not only promoted, he was also placed over the entire empire.

> *"Daniel soon showed that he could do better work than the other supervisors or the governors. Because he was so outstanding, the king considered putting him in charge of the whole empire."*
>
> -Daniel 6:3 (GNB)

Daniel made a conscious choice to be better than average. He decided he was going to display a high standard to the world and maintain that standard for himself. Daniel chose to exceed the norm and to be exceptional when everyone else around him was just doing the bare minimum. Daniel decided to outdo the competition and to go from good to great—ground to flight! Daniel positioned himself to be the King's choice!

Like Daniel, I had to make a conscious and deliberate decision to not be "average" with my goals and aspirations. I decided to work hard and remain committed to the task at hand. I graduated at the top of my high school class, finished both my B.A. and M.A.'s Degrees at Eastern Illinois University, and some years later, I completed a second Master's Degree with a 3.9 overall GPA while going through a divorce, and raising my two sons.

- Will you make excuses or will you do the required work?
- Do you see yourself as average or exceptional?
- Are you willing to follow God's plan for your life?

You must make a decision that mediocrity will only be a transitional place along your journey to a daily lifestyle of excellence!

Self-Reflection/Life Application
Chapter 2: The Enemy of Excellence is Average

1. In your own words define average:

   _____
   _____
   _____
   _____
   _____
   _____

2. In your own words define excellence:

   _____
   _____
   _____
   _____
   _____
   _____

3. Do you consider yourself average or exceptional? Explain in detail why you see yourself this way.

   _____
   _____
   _____
   _____
   _____
   _____

4. If you view yourself as average, what can you do to elevate your thinking so that you view yourself as exceptional?

_____
_____
_____
_____
_____
_____

5. In what ways do you see your gift(s) being a benefit to others and the world?

_____
_____
_____
_____
_____
_____

6. Fill in the blank with positive words that describe you.

I Am _____
I Am _____
I Am _____
I Am _____

Please Note: There are more in-depth questions provided in the accompanying workbook that will enhance your learning / growing experience.

chapter three

Distorted Image

"Opportunity is missed by most people because it is dressed in overalls and looks like work! "

Thomas A. Edison
Inventor

The image you have of yourself and how you think others perceive you will becomes a driving force or (internal navigation system) that will steer you either on the path of success or on the road that leads to failure. The Bible says in Proverbs 23:7, "For as he thinks in his heart, so is he." In other words, if you think you can be successful, you will experience success. However, if you think you can't be successful, you will fail in life until you replace the negative thinking patterns with positive thinking patterns.

The way you view or think about yourself (inwardly) has a drastic impact on your outlook (outward perception) of the world, opportunities, potential resources, and circle of influence. We have to be careful not to allow our environment(s) and the people in our environments influence or dictate the level of success we can personally experience and achieve. If you allow the wrong image or a "distorted image" to setup in your mind and take root in your thought life, that "distorted image" will begin to establish boundaries and borders that will govern and dictate your attitude, conversation, decisions, and ultimately your destiny in life. These negative images of yourself or self-defeating thoughts can bring unwanted outcomes and results in your life personally and professionally life, while negatively impacting your spiritually growth and development.

In my field of professional counseling, we use a technique called Cognitive Behavior Therapy (CBT), which is a psychotherapeutic counseling approach that helps individuals to address negative thought patterns and feelings that influence behavior(s). I have dealt with this type of challenge both personally and professionally in my efforts to establish and maintain a healthy thought-life that would foster a strong inward and outward perception of myself and others. The activities of your heart are the thoughts of your mind: if you think it, you feel it. You can't separate the two. I've often heard people say, "follow your thoughts, not your heart." The problem with this concept is the two are inseparable. The Bible says "for as he thinks in heart, so is he." What is in your heart comes out of your mouth and what comes out of your mouth is in your heart. One of the best illustrations that capture this powerful principle and demonstrates the danger of adopting a distorted image of yourself is the story I heard about the eagle who thought he was a chicken.

Your Gift is Your Leadership!

The "chicken-eagle" like so many people, could not embrace his unique gifts and talents because of mental limitations. Consequently he spent the majority of his life feeling awkward, uncomfortable, and compromising in order to gain acceptance and approval from his peers and society. The chickens, like so many people, noticed the gifting and unique abilities that the chicken-eagle possessed and instead of encouraging the chicken-eagle, they began to operate out of their own insecurities and inadequacies and began to tease, and taunt the chicken-eagle daily. The chicken-eagle internalized the rejection and hurt and became depressed, withdrawn, ashamed, and confused. Low self-esteem and learned helplessness resulted in the chicken-eagle questioning his purpose and existence. The ongoing emotional threats—whether actual trauma from continued stress and anxiety, or simply the perception of the lack of control that the chicken-eagle felt eventually impacted his cognitive belief system and sense of self. The end result for this chicken-eagle was a state of learned helplessness. The environmental factors not only established the walls of containment for the chicken-eagle; these factors shaped and framed the chicken-eagle's perception of life, self-esteem, and personal value. When I compare the differences between an eagle and a chicken, there are obvious and profound differences between the two birds.

The Eagle	The Chicken
Incredible Vision	Poor Vision
Fearless Nature	Scared & Timid
Built for High-Attitude Flight	Can't Fly
Vitality (Protected by the Law)	Short Life Span (Popular Menu Item)
Tenacious	Weak
Leader	Follower

When you compare the nature and instinct of these two birds it's literally a night and day contrast. Chickens are fearful and easily agitated. They run for shelter at the first sight of danger. Eagles, on the other hand, are fearless and not easily rattled. For example, when storms come, the eagle will not flee for shelter. Instead, the eagle actually turns his face into the storm to feel the strong wind against his face. Then, at the right time, the eagle will spread his wings, leap off of his perch, and fly directly into the storm. With his wings outstretched, he'll catch the violent updrafts caused by the storm and be immediately swept up above the clouds and into the bright sunshine.

He'll remain above the clouds until the storm blows over and the skies become calm. Now that's a long way from running around in a barnyard, making clucking sounds and waiting to become an item on the lunch menu.

In the story I shared with you, the chicken-eagle's environment framed his self-image, established mental and emotional walls of containment, and ultimately defined his destiny. The chicken-eagle died in a chicken barnyard. He was meant to soar freely, dominate the skies, and live high in the mountains. The resounding message of this story can be summed up in four points:

1. When you can't see, you doubt.

2. When you doubt, you become stagnate.

3. Stagnation stifles creativity and forward progress.

4. No creativity and forward progress=missed opportunities, growth and development.

You will only go as far as you can see yourself going in life. If you can see yourself as a doctor, you can be a doctor. If you can see yourself as a scientist, you can be a scientist. If you can see yourself as a successful business owner, you will be a successful business owner. If you can see yourself as a professional athlete, you become a professional athlete. This very principle works the same way for a positive or negative outcome. If you can't see success for your life then, you will inevitably fail and experience continued failures in your life. The level of success you will experience is based on the level of success you can see for yourself.

Identity Crisis

In general, youth and adults in today's society struggle with identity crisis. This is truly heart breaking because when we don't know our purpose, self-worth, or understand our God-given potential we become simple carbon copies of everything and everyone around us. When I was growing up on the Westside of Chicago in a poverty-stricken area, I could not see anything wrong with the crime and poverty that plagued our neighborhoods. It became a way of life for me because I had nothing to compare it against. What I saw around me at an early age is what I identified as life and the world. My perception was like the chicken-eagle. I was born in a chicken barnyard therefore, I was meant only to run and not to fly! The chicken-eagle in the story was suffering from a serious identity crisis and I was dealing with my own identity crisis. My environment did not foster self-efficacy, confidence, and personal success.

As a result of ongoing emotional trauma, continued stress, anxiety, and the lack of control in my life, like that chicken-eagle, my cognitive belief system was negatively impacted. Consequently, I operated in a state of learned helplessness. I did not feel good about myself and I did not have good thoughts about my future. I purposely surrounded myself with individuals who shared the same feelings, attitudes and belief systems. Anyone who challenged my thinking and attitude did not understand my dilemma. Therefore, I avoided these contrasting views. In my mind, I could not do anything to change my situation. The fear of failure was stronger than the desire for success. Someone once said, "In order to succeed, your desire for success should be greater than your fear of failure."

One of my favorite movies of all time is Berry Gordy's "The Last Dragon." The premise of the movie is that in order to achieve the next level of success, your desire for success has to be greater than your fear of failure. The main character, Leroy Green or (Bruce Leroy) was on a quest to become a master of kung fu. Leroy completed his final level of training with his grandmaster and was sanctioned to become a master of kung fu. However, Leroy did not feel he was qualified. Leroy felt that he needed more training, mentoring, and time before he could be considered a master of kung fu.

Leroy (like myself and the chicken-eagle) had a distorted image of himself and he lacked the necessary confidence to achieve the success he desired. As Leroy continued along his quest to obtain the "glow" or master's level in kung fu, his desire and will was consistently challenged. Leroy was teased, taunted and misunderstood, even by his family. The distorted image Leroy had of himself drove him to look externally for something that was all the while internal, (master of kung fu potential). It wasn't until a demand was placed on Leroy's potential through a climactic kung fu battle between him and his arch rival Sho'nuff that Leroy actualized the image of a master within himself. Leroy developed confidence in his ability and obtained the "glow" of mastery. Leroy not only won the battle, he gained respect and recognition as a master of kung fu.

Potential Requires Demand!

What you think is what you feel. What you feel is what you say. What you say is what you demonstrate in action. How you act will determine where you end in life. If you think you can, you will. If you think you can't, you will not. Simple, yet profound! How you think directly impacts your level of success. We have to be intentional about who we allow into our circle of influence because the wrong representation may negatively impact your thinking and set you on a course of destruction. Pastor Oral Roberts said, "If you can get a man to stand up on the inside, he will stand up on the outside." I believe this statement with all my heart. When I changed my thoughts from negative to positive, I began to surround myself with positive people. I intentionally surrounded myself with people who made similar decisions, so we could become accountability partners. I realized that in order for me to change the distorted image of myself, I had to do four things:

1. Realize that I needed to change.
2. Make a firm decision to change.
3. Evaluate my associations and environment and eliminate the "chickens."
4. Remain committed to the initial decision to change no matter how uncomfortable.

I challenge you to change your thinking! Get a positive image (picture) for your future and meditate on that image day and night until it becomes your reality. Faith is the key! Faith brings sight, strength, and endurance. Endurance is the key to manifest God's promises of peace, success, and victory.

Take a moment and reflect on your image and what you would like to see different about your life. Answer the following thought provoking questions.

Self-Reflection/Life Application
Chapter 3: Distorted Image

1. List five adjectives that describe you.

   1. _____
   2. _____
   3. _____
   4. _____
   5. _____

2. If I were to interview four of your closest friends, what would they say about you?

   _____
   _____
   _____
   _____
   _____
   _____

3. What impression about you would you like people to have after meeting you?

   _____
   _____
   _____
   _____

4. What kind of people do you attract? Chickens or eagles?

_____
_____
_____
_____

5. If you have negative thoughts, what are you doing about them?

_____
_____
_____
_____
_____
_____

Look at the simple four-step process for changing your self-image from negative to positive and complete the activities.

Step One: Realize you need to change. In one sentence admit that there are changes you need to make about your self-image to propel you into a successful life.

_____

_____

_____

_____

Step Two: <u>Make a firm decision to change.</u> Finish this sentence, "Today I will change..."

_____

_____

_____

_____

Step Three: <u>Evaluate your associations and environments and remove all chickens.</u> List any and all negative associations and environments that are potential barriers for forward progress.

negative qualities / thoughts / images of myself	the opposite of that image would be...

Step Four: <u>Stay committed to your decision to change—no matter how uncomfortable</u>. Here is where the accountability partner can make a BIG difference. Ask your accountability partner to help you remain on task and committed to the change process.

Once you change how you see yourself, you can change your associations and the direction of your life. It is your responsibility to "become" what God has ordained you to be, **SUCCESS**! Journal your process in the reflection journal note section of the workbook.

Please Note: There are more in-depth questions provided in the accompanying workbook that will enhance your learning / growing experience.

chapter four

Attitude Determines Altitude

"A positive attitude causes a chain reaction of positive thoughts, events and outcomes. It is a catalyst and it sparks extraordinary results."

Wade Boggs
Retired Professional Baseball Player

"Choosing to be positive and having a grateful attitude is going to determine how you're going to live your life."

Joel Osteen
Pastor

"Nothing can stop the man with the right mental attitude from achieving his goal; nothing on earth can help the man with the wrong mental attitude."

Raymond Chandler
Novelist

"It is not the body's posture, but the heart's attitude that counts when we pray."

Billy Graham
Evangelist

"Develop an attitude of gratitude, and give thanks for everything that happens to you, knowing that every step forward is a step toward achieving something bigger and better than your current situation."

Brian Tracy
Motivational Speaker

"Your attitude, not your aptitude, will determine your altitude."

Zig Ziglar
Motivational Speaker

I can go on and on with quotes that communicate the significance and importance of having the right attitude. In essence, your attitude is a little thing that makes a BIG difference in every area of your life.

The Bible says, in Matthew 5:5, "Blessed are the meek, for they shall inherit the earth." To be meek means to be patient, humble, mild, gentle, and submissive. This particular text of scripture is referring to having the right attitude about life, situations and circumstances. When you have the right attitude, I believe you position yourself for three things to happen:

1. Promotion

2. Recognition

3. Power of Influence

When I think about my role models – Jesus Christ, Abraham Lincoln, Martin Luther King Jr., Nelson Mandela, Jackie Robinson, and Dr. Bill Winston, they all have one thing in common, the right attitude. Each one of them experienced tremendous adversity in their efforts to manifest their vision and operate in their areas of giftedness. Not one of them folded under pressure. Instead, they met the pressure head-on and maintained a victorious attitude and as a result, they were all promoted in their respective areas and have world recognition, power, and influence.

Jesus Christ walked the earth over 2000 years ago and died so that the entire human race could be redeemed from sin and be restored into rightful fellowship with God. Jesus' ministry was predicated on him having the right attitude, and 2000 years later, we are still sharing Jesus' message of love, faith, grace, redemption, and forgiveness. Winston Churchill said it best, "Attitude is a little thing that makes a big difference."

Do You Have the Right Attitude?

Everyone has been told at one time or another that they needed an attitude adjustment. Honestly speaking, we all can benefit from a little attitude adjustment every now and then. Think about the fact that we get our cars checked out every 3,000 or 10,000 miles for oil changes or required routine maintenance. We have routine service work done in our homes when recommended by service techs, etc. If our bodies are feeling challenged, we schedule a doctor's appointment to receive a check-up. However, when we know we need an attitude adjustment, if it is our tendency to respond in one of three ways, if not all three:

1. We hesitate to act or delay our actions regarding a certain recommendation.

2. We take offense because we don't want to hear something said that challenges our attitude about our situation.

3. We respond by pointing out what's wrong with the person who shared the advice. As a result, our hearts became hardened at that moment, with the end result being a missed opportunity for personal growth and development.

"The greatest day in your life and mine is when we take total responsibility for our attitudes. That's the day we truly grow up."

John C. Maxwell
Motivational Speaker

I appreciate the connection that John Maxwell is making with regards to us taking personal responsibility for our attitudes and maturity. If you have been told that you need an attitude adjustment in order to grow to the next level in life, yet refuse to take heed, you lack maturity and refuse to grow up. This type of mindset and attitude is counterproductive to forward progress and success.

When you deny yourself the opportunity for growth and maturity, you create obstacles and hindrances that can potentially delay your success or cause you to forfeit it altogether. On the other hand, if you open your heart and mind to receive constructive criticism and then make a conscious effort to change, it is a sign of maturity that will ultimately lead to promotion, recognition and power.

Attitude is heard in your speech, seen in your appearance, and observed in your actions. People who refuse to take responsibility for their attitudes are immature and lack growth and development. An immature person's attitude is the by-product of their situation and circumstances and often their feelings are controlled and manipulated by external factors. For example, God called Moses to lead the Children of Israel from years of slavery and oppression to freedom. In order to fulfill his assignment, Moses needed to mature in faith, develop a different image of himself, and take on a new attitude about the assignment and call that God had for him to fulfill. Moses needed to get to a place where his feelings were no longer controlled and manipulated by external factors to a place where his hope; trust, and confidence was completely in God's ability to protect him and equipped him to complete the assignment. Moses needed an attitude adjustment. Moses was raised in the Pharaoh's palace as a prince and he embraced the culture of Egypt and the system of slavery. If God had not placed Moses in His "attitude-adjustment class," Moses would have led the children of Israel free and would have re-instituted the system of slavery for himself. When a

leader has the right attitude, everyone benefits according to Proverbs 29:2:

"When good people run things, everyone is glad, but when the ruler is bad, everyone groans." (MSG)

Proverbs 29:2 says that when good people run things – people with the right or "meek" attitude – everyone is glad or can benefit from this type of leadership. However, when the ruler or leader is bad (controlling, insecure, fearful, oppressive, insensitive or prejudiced), everyone groans or is sad as a result of this negative style of leadership. I have heard it said that "with great power comes great responsibility." Therefore, it is essential for anyone in a position of influence, power and leadership to have the right attitude, because the characteristic trait of effective leadership is the right attitude.

Attitude Alignment

A properly-aligned car is important to the safety and proper functioning of your vehicle from day to day. A car that has misalignment can be dangerous to drive and can cause excessive wear and tear to tires, brakes, bearings, etc. A car that is in need of an alignment will noticeably pull sharply to one side once you remove your hands from the steering wheel. Just like you can instantly tell that a car needs a wheel alignment, people can tell instantly when you need an attitude alignment. Long after your presence is gone your attitude is still felt, whether good or bad. It is important to understand that your attitude shows up before you and remains long after your departure.

If you ask this question of any random person, nine out of ten times the answer would be, "I don't have an attitude problem; I'm good!" However, I believe that once the pressures of life come (be it academics, work-related, financial situations, or relational challenges) a person's posture, outlook, speech, mindset, and sometimes his/her moral stance changes. The reason why this happens is because the individual really does not have the right attitude, and the pressure of the situation or circumstance is exposing the individual's deep feelings and hidden attitudes regarding the matter. Your attitude can place you on a trajectory of forward progress or bring you to a complete halt. Thomas Jefferson said it this way:

> ***"Nothing can stop the man with the right mental attitude from achieving his goal; nothing on earth can help the man with the wrong mental attitude."***

Your attitude affects every area of your life, including how you deal with people, situations and circumstances. Let's look at the legend of Michael Jordan for the sake of this point. We all know Michael Jordan was the greatest basketball player to ever wear gym shoes. Even my two young sons, TJ and Tim, who were not even born during the Michael Jordan championship years with the Chicago Bulls, say that Michael Jordan is the best to ever play basketball. However, did you know that Michael "Air" Jordan in 1978 tried out for the varsity basketball team at Laney High School in Wilmington, N.C. and did not make the roster?

Now, Michael could have allowed that one experience to negatively impact his attitude about the game of basketball and said to himself, "maybe, I'm not as good as I thought," or "I can't compete in this game at the next level," or even "maybe, basketball is not the sport for me!" Michael did not adopt this defeated attitude. Instead, Michael worked harder and remained committed to the process of hard work until his game improved offensively and defensively. Michael also grew a few more inches during the off season and returned the next season to claim a starting position on the basketball team. THE REST IS HISTORY!

Everything Starts and Ends with Your Attitude!

As a youngster, I did not realize how important my attitude was to myself and others. I did not realize that people could sense my attitude, whether good or bad. People responded to me based on the attitude I displayed. My siblings and I endured a lot of emotional hardships growing up. We had to face a lot of challenges at an early age, after the death of our parents. However, we all had to learn for ourselves that our attitude would determine our altitude. Once I embraced the idea of excellence and seeing myself as successful in life, I began to shape my future and say who I was and what I expected for my life. I would say the following statements about myself daily:

- "I can do anything I want to do!"
- "I can be anything I want to be!"
- "My situation and circumstance will not define me!"

- "Nobody can hold me down!"
- "Failure can't stop me!"
- "Success will not hold me!"
- "I will not allow fear to contain me!"
- "Nothing can stop me!"
- "I will be successful!"
- "I am unstoppable!"

I learned at an early age that my attitude was the key to my success, my peace, and my experiencing a positive bright future regardless of life's circumstances. My positive, upbeat attitude began to attract the right situations and the right people. The right attitude opened the right doors for me, closed the wrong doors for me and created opportunities in my life. Every person that I met… teachers, employers, and members of my church were all amazed that I was able to develop a positive attitude despite my childhood circumstances.

I remember being told that I had a teachable spirit (meekness) about myself. I was not always the smartest or most qualified person; however, I always had an attitude that "I can do anything I set my mind to and do it better than anybody else." I am thoroughly convinced that 90% of my success has come by way of my positive attitude and 10% has been my work. I believe God chooses men and women who are meek and teachable to channel His greatness into the earth. I think about Jesus Christ, Martin Luther King, Jr. Nelson Mandela, Abraham Lincoln, Jackie Robinson, and Dr. Bill Winston. The only perfect one on the list is Jesus Christ; nonetheless, if you read the Bible you will see that He also had several opportunities to develop the wrong attitude about His assignment and purpose (which was to die so that we could be redeemed from sin). Jesus was lied on, betrayed, and falsely accused. Yet, His attitude remained consistent; *"Father, forgive them, for they don't know what they are doing."* Luke 23:34

"People may hear your words, but they feel your attitude."

John C. Maxwell
Motivational Speaker

When I obtained my first job in high school, the comment I often heard was that my attitude was right for the job. I did not have any work experience, but I had the right attitude. When I was in college at Eastern Illinois University, I decided to pledge Phi Beta Sigma Fraternity, Inc. The brothers often told me that I had the right attitude to be a leader. I eventually became the president and graduate advisor for the chapter. When I decided to attend graduate school at EIU, I applied for a graduate assistantship position in the Housing Department. I was excited about the new possibilities while also nervous because I lacked experience! During the interview, I remained positive, focused, optimistic, excited and ready to take advantage of a great opportunity. Although I felt comfortable and confident, I did not know what the final outcome would be. Throughout the interview I kept hearing questions that referenced my transferable skills and work related experience for the position. The selection process was very competitive and intense. There was a big pool of candidates for only five available graduate assistantship positions.

At the conclusion of my interview, I thanked everyone for their time and I expressed a sincere gratitude for the opportunity of a lifetime. I also shared why I was the best candidate for the position. My attitude remained positive before, during, and after the interview process. After a much-anticipated wait, I was notified that I got the job!

After starting my new position, my supervisor informed me that my interview was awesome. He also pointed out the fact that my lack of experience showed during my interview. However, the determining factor for the search committees decision to hire me was my attitude. Other candidates had more relevant work experience but I had what was described as a "teachable attitude" and this was the quintessential ingredient for the job.

The right attitude will open doors for you that experience alone cannot and will not open. The right attitude will separate you from the pack, and elevate you to the top. The right attitude will cause rules and regulations to change on your behalf. The right attitude is the key to your success! The graduate assistantship gave me an income, a debt-free master's degree, supervisory experience, administrative skills and professional counseling services for the EIU students that resided in the residence halls. The right attitude created the opportunity of a lifetime for me.

Attitude Effects Vision

I once heard a story about a man who was intrigued as he walked past a construction site. So, he stopped and inquired about the end construction product. The first construction worker nonchalantly replied, "I'm just laying bricks for a building." The gentleman saw another worker working at the same construction site who was singing and smiling. So the gentleman inquired again about the project. Surprisingly, the response was different. The construction worker shared that he is laying bricks for a new state-of-the-art multi-purpose facility that will house orphans, homeless people, and victims of domestic violence. This facility will provide educational / vocational training programs, Wednesday night computer classes and Sunday church services. The second construction worker was so excited to talk about the opportunity, and to be part of such an awesome endeavor.

The gentleman noticed that he spoke with two different workers at the same construction site who both shared two totally different perspectives about the end product. The difference between the two construction workers was their individual attitudes about the roles they played in the overall project. One construction worker saw his bricks when placed together form a structure that would be used to transform lives for the better. The other construction worker saw his bricks as simple bricks. Therefore, his attitude was typical: job, nothing special, and when is the next project?

One worker could see his value and worth, the other could not. Therefore, they have contrasting perspectives because they have contrasting attitudes. You must be cognizant of the fact that your attitude affects your ability to see (vision) and without vision you will unconsciously minimize your role and not see your value and worth in the big picture. You make the difference, but you have to have the right attitude in order to see your value and worth.

"Blessed (happy, blithesome, joyous, spiritually prosperous with life joy and satisfaction in God's favor and salvation, regardless of their outward conditions) are the meek (the mild, patient, longsuffering), for they shall inherit the earth."

- Matthew 5:5 AMP

Your attitude will determine your altitude! So, remember if you want to fly high in life, it's imperative to have the right (meek) attitude. You will only go as high in life as your attitude allows you to go. Don't let a little thing (attitude) stop you from experiencing a BIG future of success, joy, prosperity, and satisfaction.

Self-Reflection/Life Application
Chapter 4: Attitude Determines Altitude

1. Review the quotes at the beginning of chapter four in the book and identify the one quote that resonates with you. Write the quote down and share why this quote is impactful to you.

_____
_____
_____
_____
_____

2. Now, write your own quote or personal affirmation that best reflects your attitude and perspective on life.

_____
_____
_____
_____
_____
_____
_____
_____

3. When you have the right attitude, you position yourself for three things to happen in your life. List these three things.

1. _____
2. _____
3. _____

4. Who is your role model? What is the attitude of this individual about life? What adversity did this individual have to overcome to achieve success?

_____
_____
_____
_____
_____
_____

5. Has anyone ever told you that you should improve your attitude? Did you respond in a negative way or in a positive way? Take a moment and journal your thoughts about the conversation or incident.

_____
_____
_____
_____

_____
_____
_____
_____
_____

6. Do you think you have a mindset that is open towards correction? (circle one)

YES   NO

Please Note: There are more in-depth questions provided in the accompanying workbook that will enhance your learning/growing experience.

chapter five

Finish the work

"When we make progress quickly, it feeds our emotions. Then, when there's a period of waiting or we hit a plateau, we find out how committed we really are and whether we're going to see things through to the finish or quit."

Joyce Meyer
Evangelist / Author

The one thing that I've come to understand in life is that whatever you want is going to require work in order to obtain it. This principle is understood and embraced by successful people in all walks of life: business, professional sports, media, technology, politics, ministry, entrepreneurship, and entertainment. Work is the quintessential ingredient that is required to have a finished product. There is absolutely no other way around the process of work! Like Joyce Meyer said we make some quick progress, then we are feeling good about ourselves. However, the work remains unfinished until we complete the required process.

The Process Equals The Product

Process is the commitment - work is the product! A great illustration of this point is the Nike commercial, "Failure." This commercial is about Michael Jordan getting out of his vehicle at the United Center in Chicago and walking through the hallways reflecting on his past failures: 9,000 missed shots, 300 lost games, and 26 missed game-winning shots. Michael concludes the commercial with this very powerful statement, "I've failed over, and over, and over again in my life and that is why I succeed."

Failure Is the Other Side of Success

Michael did not allow his failures to stop his drive to succeed. Michael Jordan, like anyone else who has achieved anything great in life, understood the value and importance of the finished work.

"Defeat doesn't finish a man, quit does. A man is not finished when he's defeated. He's finished when he quits."

Richard M. Nixon
Former United States President

Michael Jordan did not allow defeat to stop him in his quest for greatness. Jordan with all his success had to go through the process, or through his period of waiting in order to develop the necessary confidence to take the next winning game shot after 26 missed attempts. Don't stop during the process; go through the process!

It's during the process that we have a tendency to hit a plateau. Then, we find out how committed we really are and whether we're going to stay the course to **FINISH** what we started.

In order to finish the work, we have to commit to the process. This is usually an uncomfortable time because it requires personal growth and development. The process is a time when there is no fanfare, lights, or cameras- only action! These are moments when it's only you, your God, and your dreams. The process brings with it moments of silence, time for reflection, and adjustments. This is a private, upfront, in your face, self-check season where development of character, image, integrity, attitude, will, desire, and commitment are at the forefront. In my opinion, the process is most important because it is a transformational time that will determine your level of success or depth of failure.

God Is With You!

The process is much like a modern day "wilderness" experience because it is designed to expose what is in our hearts and minds while preparing us for the next level of power and victory. Sometimes, we think we know and really don't. God who loves us all will not allow us to be caught off guard and made a shame. Therefore, He will allow us to have personal wilderness experiences to expose and show us the matters of our hearts. When we see clearly, we can grow and God can purify our hearts and qualify us for next level promotion. Nobody wants to go into the wilderness or experience the process because we all want the end result without the blood, sweat, and tears. Let's be honest, the process or wilderness is extremely uncomfortable! God uses the process or wilderness experience to purge for power. The process qualifies us to become the product! The Bible says, in Deuteronomy 8:2:

> *"And you shall (earnestly) remember all the way which the Lord your God led you these forty years in the wilderness, to humble you and to prove you, to know what was in your (mind and heart...)"*

God allowed Moses, Joseph, Paul, Peter, Joshua, the children of Israel, and Jesus to go through a wilderness experience before they could operate in their assignment and fulfill their purpose. Joseph's process or wilderness experience continued in Genesis Chapters 39-41 where Joseph was wrongfully accused by his master's wife and put into prison for a crime he didn't commit. While in prison, God continue to shape and mold Joseph's character, leadership, and integrity. Joseph's next level of promotion came in Genesis 41:39-41. The Bible says,

> *"And Pharaoh said to Joseph, Forasmuch as (your) God has shown you all this, there*

is nobody as intelligent and discreet and understanding and wise as you are. You shall have charge over my house, and all my people shall be governed according to your word (with reverence, submission, and obedience). Only in matters of the throne will I be greater than you are. Then Pharaoh said to Joseph, See I have set you over all the land of Egypt."

The wilderness experience allows you to come face-to-face with your hidden heart issues and it also provides an opportunity to deal with your issues without shame. The wilderness experience is a personal, self-check season in your life where you have the opportunity to develop in the following areas: character, self-image, integrity, maturity, attitude, endurance, forgiveness, and your level of commitment to your own personal success. Joseph had plenty of opportunities, just like you and I will have, to give-up, embrace un-forgiveness or quit on life because things are not working out according to plan. The process is where you make the decision to succeed or fail!

The wilderness experience is a time in which God can expand us in areas where growth is necessary, develop us in areas where development is essential, and expose us to His unfailing LOVE and His commitment to OUR success. The Bible says in Philippians 1:6, **"And I am certain that God, who began the good work within you, will continue His work until it is finally finished on the day when Christ Jesus returns." (NLT)**

This scripture is encouraging to me because it tells me that I don't have to bear the pressure of completing my assignment alone. God, who gave the assignment (purpose), is obligated to assist you and I because He began the good work within us, and He will stay with us until it is finally finished! What you were born to do is what God intended for you to finish.

Unfinished Work or Finished Work: What Will Be Your Legacy?

Every person has a desire to fulfill their dreams and aspirations. Why? – Because you were born to finish! You were born a winner! The blueprint for success is within you and work provides the opportunity to manifest your potential from the inside – out. You have a work to do but more importantly, a work to bring to completion! God has placed purpose and potential on the inside of you. It's your responsibility to start and finish your race so that you can leave a legacy of success, fulfillment, endurance, courage, faith, integrity, commitment, and a finished work for your children to model and demonstrate to their children. It's about your legacy and what that legacy says about you. Will it say that you are the type of person who starts and never finishes, or will it say that whatever you started, you completed? God has equipped you with everything you need— Now, finish the work!

Become a Graveyard Digger

When I was in my senior year of high school, I remember having one of those father/son conversations with my Uncle Frank about my future plans. Uncle Frank asked me what I wanted to be and why was I going to college? My response was that I wanted to become a lawyer or businessman of some sort. I wasn't 100% sure of my career path but I knew that I wanted to attend college after graduating high school. To my surprise, my uncle's response was, "Why... Why would you want to go to college to become a lawyer? That's trouble!" He continued to say,

"Lawyers get caught in too much mess! They are corrupt and they don't make enough money to have to deal with other people and their problems! Why don't you skip college and get a job like me. Earn some good honest money working at the graveyard! Dwayne, what you are talking about is not realistic for black people. Become a graveyard digger!"

My uncle didn't mean any harm when he tried to convince me to forfeit an opportunity to attend college and pursue a full time job working at the cemetery with him. He was just speaking out of his own personal barnyard experience. The irony of the situation is that I wanted to get out into the world and be around people who were pursuing their dreams and aspirations. Yet, my uncle was trying to convince me to remain in a place of starvation, stagnation, and death: The Graveyard!

I once heard Myles Munroe say that the graveyard was the richest place in the earth because of the wasted gifts, talents, and dreams that were never actualized. The graveyard is a place filled with unwritten books, unfulfilled visions, aspirations, and potential. I did not want to be a contributor to this place of unfilled potential; therefore, I decided against my uncle's advice and pursued college after graduating from high school.

That conversation with my uncle taught me a great lesson. It helped me to understand that you must be careful, mindful, and observant of whom you share your dreams with. The person can be a family member, co-worker, or close friend who genuinely has your best interest at heart. People, though, can only speak out of their own personal experiences, and if they have a legacy of unfulfilled work, that is all they can share with you. Don't get angry with them, but understand their mindset and attitude.

My parents died when I was a kid and as a result of that void in my life, I never had the opportunity to benefit from them operating in their gifts and finishing what they were born to do. Unfinished work leads to more unfinished work. Whenever I felt depressed, devalued, worthless, and insignificant, it was a direct result of not understanding my purpose and how important diligence, commitment, focus and finished work impacted my self-image. To every parent that reads this book, please model for your children what you want them to experience in their lives. If you display a lifestyle that hard work pays, always maintaining a life of integrity, and finishing what you start. People will not only see your work, they will follow your example of "finished work."

Finish the Work

Unfinished work is like missing pieces to a puzzle. There is no real appreciation for the picture because the image is distorted due to missing pieces. If the puzzle is not finished, the picture is incomplete; if the picture is incomplete, the picture has no value or worth. Just like the puzzle that holds no value because of the missing piece, our personal lives can appear to be without lasting impact when we do not finish our work. The Message Bible makes it very clear and simple in II Corinthians 8:11:

"The best thing you can do right now is to finish what you started last year and not let those good intentions grow stale. Your heart's been in the right place all along. You've got what it takes to finish it up, so go to it."

Playing to Win

When I was a youngster, winning was everything to me. I was told though "Dwayne, it does not matter if you win or lose; it is how you play the game." I understand now that I did not understand the value of this statement. Here is the message; you have prepared yourself, you have the right attitude, and have put forth your best effort, therefore you are a winner! When I ran the Chicago Rock-n-Roll half-marathon a few years ago, it was the greatest feeling in the world to cross that finish line. I did not break nor did I set a new record for time of completion. I did not even finish my personal training course time. But, I finished the race and I'm classified as a Marathon Finisher!

Victories come in all shapes and sizes and every situation is personal. If the victory does not come right away, it's okay. Stay the course! Continue to say the following about yourself:

- I am victorious!
- I am a winner!
- I am a finisher!
- I will do what I was born to do!
- God is with me!

Keep in mind that when I speak about winning, I am talking about you finishing the work. The work in front of you can be any of the following: completing your GED, graduating high school or college, getting a job, or pursuing the career of your choice, starting a business, being a better parent to your children, being a better spouse, starting a church, or writing a book. Whatever fulfills you and adds quality of life to those around you, links you directly to your purpose, your calling, your assignment, and your work.

Discovery of Self Leads to Discovery For Others

I remember looking into the eyes of my GED students from my educational and vocational programs and I saw confidence, pride, joy, fulfillment, growth and accomplishment – finished work! These students were elated and excited about their futures. Why? Because another piece of the puzzle was now in place and they were actualizing their dreams. They began to share with me how they planned to attend college or trade school in order to better prepare themselves for the next level of work in their lives.

> *"Your work is going to fill a large part of your life, and the only way to be truly satisfied is to do what you believe is great work. The only way to do great work is to love what you do."*
>
> *Steve Jobs*
> *Inventor/Founder of Apple*

The students understood the time commitment necessary, felt good about what they were doing, and loved the road they were now on that would lead to success.

Inside of each one of us are dreams, talents, skills, abilities, unlimited potential and power. You were born for a special assignment that only you can do. Think about this; there are over 7 billion people in the earth and not one person has the same eye retina, fingerprint or spiral of DNA. No other person possesses your unique set of gifts, talents or dreams. Just as no two snowflakes are alike, you are like no one else on this entire earth. NOBODY has your God-given potential! Your unique expression of gifts and talents qualifies you to be in a class all by yourself, without competition. Your potential defines both your destiny and your life calling. Nobody can operate in your unique individual calling or assignment. This gift or ability that God has given you was uniquely crafted and designed for you only. When God made you, He "broke the mold."

Self-Reflection/Life Application
Chapter 5: Finish The Work

1. The process is the _____, work is the _____.

2. The writer says that "failure is the other side of success." What does this mean to you?

   _____
   _____
   _____
   _____
   _____

3. Think about the Michael Jordan quote, "I've failed over, and over, and over again in my life and that is why I succeed." Why is this significant and how can you apply this principle to your life?

   _____
   _____
   _____
   _____
   _____

4. Reflecting on your failures, what have you learned about yourself and how can you turn these failures into successes?

_____
_____
_____
_____
_____
_____

5. The writer talks about the "wilderness experience." Explain the writer's perspective of the "wilderness experience" as it pertains to a season in one's life.

_____
_____
_____
_____
_____
_____

6. Why is legacy so important? What type of legacy will you leave for your children?

_____
_____
_____

_____

_____

_____

Please Note: There are more in-depth questions provided in the accompanying workbook that will enhance your learning/growing experience.

chapter six

The Product

"The end of something is better than its beginning."
Ecclesiastes 7:8 (NLT)

What spectacular things are you holding back from the world?

What do you dream about?

What do you talk about?

What do you want to be in life?

What burning desire(s) do you have?

Your God-given potential is limitless!

You are AWESOME!

BECOME The Product YOU WERE CREATED TO BE!

Every person and experience that you have has directly impacted, shaped and influenced the person you are today. This is a part of your process! You are the sum total of your life experiences and relationships. That is your product! If you are not happy with your product, change your process!

The Process Equals the Product

Success is inside you and it's your responsibility to work success from the inside out! Release your potential for greatness - **Become the "product" God ordained you to be!**

> *"Nothing can stop the man with the right mental attitude from achieving his goal; nothing on earth can help the man with the wrong mental attitude."*
>
> *Thomas Jefferson*
> *Former President of the United States*

The Process Equals The Product - Goal Setting

I have three very important questions for you to answer:

1. Do you know what you want in life?

2. Do you understand the process that is required to obtain your personal, professional, and financial dreams?

3. Have your written your vision and made it plain? If not, why not?

4. My Ultimate Goal:

5. What three things can I do right now that will position me to obtain my goal?

   1.
   2.
   3.

To further develop your goals and organizational skills, the Life Application Workbook is highly recommended.

Action Plan

Short-term Plan (1 month – 3 months)

1.

2.

3.

Mid-term Plan (3 months – 9 months)

1.

2.

3.

Long-term Plan (9 months – 3 years)

1.

2.

3.

Goal:

Date of completion:

Say Something!

Death and Life Are in the Power of Your Tongue!

Introduction to Salvation

"For God so loved the world that he gave His only begotten son, that whosoever believeth in Him should not perish, but have everlasting life. For God sent not His Son into the world to condemn the world; but that the world through Him might be saved."

I have six very important questions to ask:

1. Have you made Jesus Christ your personal Lord and Savior? (Romans 10:9-10)

2. Did you know that Jesus came to destroy the works of the devil in your life? (1 John 3:8)

3. Did you know that Jesus is the Light of the world? (John 9:5)

4. If you died today, where would you spend eternity – in heaven or hell? (Romans 10:9)

5. Did you know that God so loved the world that he gave His only begotten Son so that we would have life and not death? (John 3:16)

6. Did you know that Jesus loves you? (John 15:9)

Jesus Christ is Lord

If you have already received Jesus Christ as your personal Lord and Savior, praise the Lord! You can be assured that if you died today you will go directly to heaven to be with the Father. If you have not confessed Jesus Christ as your personal Lord and Savior, I invite you to say this very simple prayer:

> "Lord Jesus, I come to you now just as I am. You know my life and You know how I've lived. I repent of my sins. I believe Jesus Christ is the Son of God and He died on the cross for my sins. On the third day, He was raised from the dead. Lord Jesus I ask that you come into my heart. Live Your life in me and through me. From this day forward I belong to You! I renounce the devil and receive Jesus Christ as my new Lord and Savior! Thank You Lord for adopting me into your family. I am a new creature in Christ and old things have passed away in life in Jesus Name!"

Bio Sketches

Notable People In History

DR. JOHN AVANZINI (Born in Paramaribo, Suriname, South America on May 21, 1936) is an American televangelist and "Word of Faith" Bible teacher who preaches a message of financial prosperity. Avanzini who was raised in Lake Jackson, Texas, has his present ministry, which he began in 1988, based in nearby Corpus Christi, Texas. Central to his teachings is his claim that Jesus and his followers were rich and that the believer is promised wealth. He received his doctorate degree from Baptist Christian University in Shreveport, Louisiana. He has five grown children one of whom, David Avanzini, happens to run his ministry.

WADE ANTHONY BOGGS (Born June 15, 1958) is an American former professional baseball third baseman. He spent his 18-year baseball career primarily with the Boston Red Sox, but also played for the

New York Yankees, with whom he won his only World Series, and Tampa Bay Devil Rays, with whom he recorded his 3,000th hit. His hitting in the 1980s and 1990s made him a perennial contender for American League batting titles. He is 33rd on the list of career leaders for batting average among Major League Baseball players with a minimum of 1,000 plate appearances. Boggs was elected to the Red Sox Hall of Fame in 2004, and the Baseball Hall of Fame in 2005.

With 12 straight All-Star appearances, Boggs is third only to Brooks Robinson and George Brett in number of consecutive appearances as a third baseman. In 1999, he ranked number 95 on the Sporting News list of the 100 Greatest Baseball Players, and was a nominee for the Major League Baseball All-Century Team. Boggs, a 1976 graduate of Plant High School in Tampa, Florida, currently resides in the Tampa Palms neighborhood of Tampa.

KOBE "BEAN" BRYANT (Born August 23, 1978), nicknamed the "Black Mamba", is an American professional basketball player for the Los Angeles Lakers of the National Basketball Association (NBA). He entered the NBA directly from high school, and has played for the Lakers his entire career, winning five NBA championships. Bryant is a 16-time All-Star, 15-time member of the All-NBA Team, and 12-time member of the All-Defensive team. As of March 2013, he ranks third and fourth on the league's all-time postseason scoring and all-time regular season scoring lists, respectively.

Bryant enjoyed a successful high school basketball career at Lower Merion High School, where he was recognized as the top high school basketball player in the country. He declared his eligibility for the NBA Draft upon graduation, and was selected with the 13th overall pick in the 1996 NBA Draft by the Charlotte Hornets, then traded to the Los Angeles Lakers. As a rookie, Bryant earned himself a reputation as a high-flyer and a fan favorite by winning the 1997 Slam Dunk Contest.

Bryant and Shaquille O'Neal led the Lakers to three consecutive championships from 2000 to 2002. A heated feud between the duo and a loss in the 2004 NBA Finals was followed by O'Neal's trade from the Lakers after the 2003–04 season. Following O'Neal's departure Bryant became the cornerstone of the Los Angeles Lakers franchise. He led the NBA in scoring during the 2005–06 and 2006–07 seasons, setting numerous scoring records in the process. In 2006, Bryant scored a career-high 81 points against the Toronto Raptors, the second most points scored in a single game in

NBA history, second only to Wilt Chamberlain's 100-point game in 1962. He was awarded the regular season's Most Valuable Player Award (MVP) in 2008. After losing in the 2008 NBA Finals, Bryant led the Lakers to two consecutive championships in 2009 and 2010, earning the NBA Finals MVP Award on both occasions.

At 34 years and 104 days of age, Bryant became the youngest player in league history to reach 30,000 career points. He is also the all-time leading scorer in Lakers franchise history. Since his second year in the league, Bryant has been selected to start every All-Star Game. He has won the All-Star MVP Award four times (2002, 2007, 2009, and 2011), tying him for the most All Star MVP Awards in NBA history. At the 2008 and 2012 Summer Olympics, he won gold medals as a member of the USA national team. Sporting News and TNT named Bryant the top NBA player of the 2000s.

GEORGE WASHINGTON CARVER (Circa January 1864 – January 5, 1943), was an American scientist, botanist, educator, and inventor. The exact day and year of his birth are unknown; he is believed to have been born into slavery in Missouri in January 1864.

Carver's reputation is based on his research into and promotion of alternative crops to cotton, such as peanuts, soybeans and sweet potatoes, which aided nutrition for farm families. He wanted poor farmers to grow alternative crops both as a source of their own food and as a source of other products to improve their quality of life. The most popular of his 44 practical bulletins for farmers contained 105 food recipes using peanuts. He also developed and promoted about 100 products made from peanuts that were useful for the house and farm, including cosmetics, dyes, paints, plastics, gasoline, and nitroglycerin. He received numerous honors for his work, including the Spingarn Medal of the NAACP. During the Reconstruction-era South, monoculture of cotton depleted the soil in many areas. In the early 20th century, the boll weevil destroyed much of the cotton crop, and planters and farm workers suffered. Carver's work on peanuts was intended to provide an alternative crop.

He was recognized for his many achievements and talents. In 1941, Time magazine dubbed Carver a "Black Leonardo."

RAYMOND THORNTON CHANDLER (July 23, 1888–March 26,1959) was an American novelist and screenwriter. In 1932, at age forty-four, Raymond Chandler decided to become a detective fiction writer after losing his job as an oil company executive during the Depression. His first short story, "Blackmailers Don't Shoot," was published in 1933 in Black Mask, a popular pulp magazine. His first novel, *The Big Sleep*, was published in 1939. In addition to his short stories, Chandler published only seven full novels during his lifetime (Although an eighth in progress at his death was completed by Robert B. Parker).

All but *Playback* have been made into motion pictures, some several times. In the year before he died, he was elected president of the Mystery Writers of America. He died on March 26, 1959, in La Jolla, California.

Chandler had an immense stylistic influence on American popular literature. He is considered by many to be a founder, along with Dashiell Hammett, James M. Cain and other Black Mask writers, of the hard-boiled school of detective fiction. His protagonist, Philip Marlowe, along with

Hammett's Sam Spade, is considered by some to be synonymous with "private detective," both having been played on screen by Humphrey Bogart, whom many considered to be the quintessential Marlowe.

Some of Chandler's novels are considered important literary works, and three are often considered masterpieces: *Farewell, My Lovely* (1940), *The Little Sister* (1949), *and The Long Goodbye* (1953). The *Long Goodbye* is praised within an anthology of American crime stories as "arguably the first book since Hammett's The Glass Key, published more than twenty years earlier, to qualify as a serious and significant mainstream novel that just happened to possess elements of mystery."

JESUS (7–2 BC to 30–33 AD), also referred to as "Jesus of Nazareth," is the central figure of Christianity (the world's largest religion), whom the teachings of most Christian denominations hold to be the Son of God. Christianity regards Jesus as the awaited  Messiah of the Old Testament and refers to him as Jesus Christ, a name that is also used in non-Christian contexts. various portraits of the historical Jesus, which often depict him as having one or more of the following roles: the leader of an apocalyptic movement, Messiah, a charismatic healer, a sage and philosopher, or an egalitarian social reformer. Scholars have correlated the New Testament accounts with non-Christian historical records to arrive at an estimated chronology of Jesus' life. The most widely used calendar era in the world (abbreviated as "AD", alternatively referred to as "CE"), counts from a medieval estimate of the birth year of Jesus.

Christians believe that Jesus has a "unique significance" in the world. Christian doctrines include the beliefs that Jesus was conceived by the Holy Spirit, was born of a virgin, performed miracles, founded the Church, died by crucifixion as a sacrifice to achieve atonement, rose from the dead, and ascended into heaven, whence he will return. The great majority of Christians worship Jesus as the incarnation of God the Son, the second of three persons of a Divine Trinity. A few Christian groups reject Trinitarianism, wholly or partly, as non-scriptural.

In Islam, Jesus (commonly transliterated as Isa) is considered one of God's important prophets and the Messiah. To Muslims, Jesus is a bringer of scripture and the child of a virgin birth, but neither divine nor the victim of crucifixion. Judaism rejects the belief that Jesus was the awaited Messiah, arguing that he did not fulfill the Messianic prophecies in the Tanakh.

SIR WINSTON LEONARD SPENCER-CHURCHILL, (November 30, 1874 – January 24, 1965) was a British politi- cian who was the Prime Minister of the United Kingdom from 1940 to 1945 and again from 1951 to 1955. Widely regarded as one of the greatest wartime leaders of the 20th century, Churchill was also an officer in the British Army, a historian, a writer, and an artist. He is the only British Prime Minister to have won the Nobel Prize in Lit- erature, and was the first person to be made an honorary citizen of the United States

FREDERICK DOUGLASS (Born Frederick Augustus Washington Bailey, circa February 1818 – February 20, 1895) was an African-American social reform- er, orator, writer and statesman. After escaping from slavery, he became a leader of the abo-  litionist movement, gaining note for his dazzling oratory and incisive antislavery writing. He stood as a living counter-example to slaveholders' arguments that slaves did not have the intellectual capacity to function as independent American citizens. Many Northerners also found it hard to believe that such a great orator had been a slave.

Douglass wrote several autobiographies, eloquently describing his experiences in slavery in his 1845 autobiography, Narrative of the Life of Frederick Douglass, an American Slave, which became influential in its support for abolition. He wrote two more autobiographies, with his last, Life and Times of Frederick Douglass, published in 1881 and covering events through and after the Civil War. After the Civil War, Douglass remained active in the United States' struggle to reach its potential as a "land of the free." Douglass actively supported women's suffrage. Without his approval, he became the first African American nominated for Vice President of the United States as the running mate of Victoria Woodhull on the impracticable and small Equal Rights Party ticket. Douglass held multiple public offices.

Douglass was a firm believer in the equality of all people, whether black, female, Native American, or recent immigrant, famously quoted as saying, "I would unite with anybody to do right and with nobody to do wrong."

CHARLES RICHARD DREW (June 3, 1904 – April 1, 1950) was an American physician, surgeon, and medical researcher. He researched in the field of blood transfusions, developing improved techniques for blood storage, and applied his expert knowledge to developing large-scale blood banks early in World War II. This allowed medics to save thousands of lives of the Allied forces. The research and development aspect of his blood storage work is disputed. As the most prominent African-American in the field, Drew protested against the practice of racial segregation in the donation of blood, as it lacked scientific foundation, an action which cost him his job.

THOMAS ALVA EDISON (February 11, 1847 – October 18, 1931) was an American inventor and businessman. He developed many devices that greatly influenced life around the world, including the phonograph, the motion picture camera, and a

long-lasting, practical electric light bulb. Dubbed "The Wizard of Menlo Park", he was one of the first inventors to apply the principles of mass production and large-scale teamwork to the process of invention, and because of that, he is often credited with the creation of the first industrial research laboratory.

Edison was a prolific inventor, holding 1,093 US patents in his name, as well as many patents in the United Kingdom, France, and Germany. More significant than the number of Edison's patents, are the impacts of his inventions, because Edison not only invented things, his inventions established major new industries world-wide, notably, electric light and power utilities, sound recording and motion pictures. Edison's inventions contributed to mass communication and, in particular, telecommunications. These included a stock ticker, a mechanical vote recorder, a battery for an electric car, electrical power, recorded music, and motion pictures.

His advanced work in these fields was an outgrowth of his early career as a telegraph operator. Edison developed a system of electric-power generation and distribution to homes, businesses, and factories – a crucial development in the modern industrialized world. His first power station was on Pearl Street in Manhattan, New York.

MOHANDAS KARAMCHAND GANDHI (October 2, 1869 – January 30, 1948) was the preeminent leader of Indian nationalism in British - ruled India. Employing nonviolent civil disobedience, Gandhi led India to independence and inspired movements for civil rights and freedom across the world. The honorific Mahatma (Sanskrit: "high- souled", "venerable")—applied to him first in 1914 in South Africa,— is now used worldwide. He is also called Bapu (Gujarati: endearment for "father", "papa") in India.

Gandhi was born and raised in a Hindu, merchant caste, family in coastal Gujarat, western India, and trained in law at the Inner Temple, London. Gandhi first employed nonviolent civil disobedience as an expatriate lawyer in South Africa, in the resident Indian community's struggle for civil rights. After his return to India in 1915, he set about organizing peasants, farmers, and urban laborers to protest against excessive land-tax and discrimination. Assuming leadership of the Indian National Congress in 1921, Gandhi led nationwide campaigns for easing poverty, expanding women's rights, building religious and ethnic amity, ending untouchability, but above all for achieving Swaraj or self-rule.

Gandhi famously led Indians in challenging the British-imposed salt tax with the 400 km (250 mi) Dandi Salt March in 1930, and later in calling for the British to Quit India in 1942. He was imprisoned for many years, upon many occasions, in both South Africa and India. Gandhi attempted to practice nonviolence and truth in all situations, and advocated that others do the same. He lived modestly in a self-sufficient residential community and wore the traditional Indian dhoti and shawl, woven with yarn hand spun on a charkha. He ate simple vegetarian food, and undertook long fasts as means of both self-purification and social protest.

WILLIAM HENRY "BILL" GATES III (born October 28, 1955) is an American business magnate, investor, program- mer, inventor, and philanthropist. Gates is the former chief executive and chairman of Microsoft, the world's largest personal-computer software company, which he co-founded with Paul Allen.

He is consistently ranked in the Forbes list of the world's wealthiest people and was the wealthiest overall from 1995 to 2009—excluding 2008, when he was ranked third; in 2011 he was the wealthiest American and the world's second wealthiest person. According to the Bloomberg Billionaires List, Gates is the world's richest person in 2013, a position that he last held on the list in 2007.

During his career at Microsoft, Gates held the positions of CEO and chief software architect, and remains the largest individual shareholder, with 6.4 percent of the common stock. He has also authored and co-authored several books.

Gates is one of the best-known entrepreneurs of the personal computer revolution. Gates has been criticized for his business tactics, which have been considered anti-competitive, an opinion which has in some cases been upheld by judicial courts. In the later stages of his career, Gates has pursued a number of philanthropic endeavors, donating large amounts of money to various charitable organizations and scientific research programs through the Bill & Melinda Gates Foundation, established in 2000.

Gates stepped down as chief executive officer of Microsoft in January 2000. He remained as chairman and created the position of chief software architect for himself. In June 2006, Gates announced that he would be transitioning from full-time work at Microsoft to part-time work, and full-time work at the Bill & Melinda Gates Foundation. He gradually transferred his duties to

Ray Ozzie, chief software architect, and Craig Mundie, chief research and strategy officer. Gates' last full-time day at Microsoft was June 27, 2008. He stepped down as chairman of Microsoft in February 2014, taking on a new post as technology advisor to support newly appointed CEO Satya Nadella.

BERRY GORDY, JR. (Born November 28, 1929) is an American record producer, and songwriter. He is best known as the founder of the Motown record label, as well as its many subsidiaries.

Gordy reinvested the profits from his songwriting success into producing. In 1957, he discovered The Miracles (originally known as The Matadors) and began building a portfolio of successful artists. In 1959, at Miracles leader Smokey Robinson's encouragement,

Gordy borrowed $800 from his family to create R&B label Tamla Records. On January 21, 1959, "Come To Me" by Marv Johnson was issued as Tamla 101. United Artists Records picked up "Come To Me" for national distribution, as well as Johnson's more successful follow-up records (such as "You Got What It Takes", co-produced and co-written by Gordy). Berry's next release was the only 45 ever issued on his Rayber label, and it featured Wade Jones with an unnamed female back-up group. The record did not sell well and is now one of the rarest issues from the Motown stable. Berry's third release was "Bad Girl" by The Miracles, and was the first-ever release for the Motown record label. "Bad Girl" was a solid hit in 1959 after Chess Records picked it up. Barrett Strong's "Money (That's What I Want)" initially appearing on Tamla and then charted on Gordy's sister's label, Anna Records, in February 1960. The Miracles' hit "Shop Around" peaked at No. 1 on the national R&B charts in late 1960 and at No. 2 on the Billboard pop charts on January 16, 1961 (#1 Pop, Cash Box), which established Motown as an independent company worthy of notice. Later in 1961, The Marvelettes' "Please Mr. Postman" made it to the top of both charts.

In 1960, Gordy signed an unknown named Mary Wells who became the fledgling label's first star, with Smokey Robinson penning her hits "You Beat Me to the Punch", "Two Lovers", and "My Guy". The Tamla and Motown labels were then merged into a new company Motown Record Corporation, which was incorporated on April 14, 1959. Gordy's gift for identifying and bringing together musical talent, along with the careful management of his artists' public image, made Motown initially a major national and then international success. Over the next decade, he signed such artists as

The Supremes, Marvin Gaye, The Temptations, Jimmy Ruffin, The Contours, The Four Tops, Gladys Knight & the Pips, The Commodores, The Velvelettes, Martha and the Vandellas, Stevie Wonder and The Jackson 5.

WILLIAM FRANKLIN "BILLY" GRAHAM, JR. (born November 7, 1918) is an American evangelical Christian evangelist, ordained as a Southern Baptist minister, who rose to celebrity status in 1949 reaching a core constituency of white, middle-class, moderately conservative Protestants. He held large indoor and outdoor rallies; sermons were broadcast on radio and television, some still being re-broadcast today.

Graham was a spiritual adviser to several Presidents; he was particularly close to Dwight D. Eisenhower, Lyndon Johnson (who was considered to be one of Graham's closest friends) and Richard Nixon. During the civil rights movement, he began to support integrated seating for his revivals and crusades; in 1957 he invited Martin Luther King, Jr. to preach jointly at a revival in New York City. Graham bailed King out of jail in the 1960s when he was arrested in demonstrations.

Graham operates a variety of media and publishing outlets. According to his staff, more than 3.2 million people have responded to the invitation at Billy Graham Crusades to "accept Jesus Christ as their personal savior". As of 2008, Graham's estimated lifetime audience, including radio and television broadcasts, topped 2.2 billion.

Graham has repeatedly been on Gallup's list of most admired men and women. He has appeared on the list 55 times since 1955 (including 49 consecutive years), more than any other individual in the world. Grant Wacker reports: By the middle 1960s, he had become the "Great Legitimator" ...His presence conferred sanctity on events, authority on presidents, acceptability on wars, desirability on decency, [and] shame on indecency...By the middle 1970s, many deemed him "America's pastor."

LEBRON RAYMONE JAMES (Born December 30, 1984), nicknamed "King James", is an American professional basketball player for the Cleveland Cavaliers of the National Basketball Association (NBA). Standing at 6ft 8in (2.03 m) and weighing 250 lb (113 kg), he has played the small forward and power forward positions. James has won two NBA championships (2012, 2013), four NBA Most

Valuable Player Awards (2009, 2010, 2012, 2013), two NBA Finals MVP Awards (2012, 2013), two Olympic gold medals (2008, 2012), an NBA scoring title (2008), and the NBA Rookie of the Year Award (2004). He has also been selected to 12 NBA All-Star teams, 11 All-NBA teams, and six All-Defensive teams, and is the Cavaliers' all-time leading scorer.

James played high school basketball at St. Vincent–St. Mary High School in his home-town of Akron, Ohio, where he was highly promoted in the national media as a future NBA superstar. After graduating, he was selected with the first overall pick in the 2003 NBA Draft by the Cavaliers. James led Cleveland to the franchise's first Finals appearance in 2007, losing to the San Antonio Spurs in a sweep. In 2010, he left the Cavaliers for the Heat in a highly publicized free agency period. In his first season in Miami, the Heat reached the Finals but lost to the Dallas Mavericks. James won his first championship in 2012 when Miami defeated the Oklahoma City Thunder, being named the Finals MVP Award for his play. In 2013, he led the Heat on a 27-game winning streak, the second longest in league history. Miami also won their second consecutive title and he repeated as Finals MVP. His career achievements and leadership role during Miami's 2012 and 2013 championship runs have led many basketball analysts to consider him the best player in the NBA today.

Off the court, James has accumulated considerable wealth and fame as a result of numerous endorsement deals. His public life has been the subject of much scrutiny, and he has been ranked as one of America's most popular, disliked, and influential athletes. He has also been featured in books, documentaries, and television commercials, and has hosted the ESPY Awards and Saturday Night Live.

THOMAS JEFFERSON (April 13, 1743 – July 4, 1826) was an American Founding Father, the principal author of the Declaration of Independence (1776) and the third President of the United States (1801–1809). He was a spokesman for democracy and the rights of man with worldwide influence. At the beginning of the American Revolution, he served in the Continental Congress, representing Virginia and then served as a wartime Governor of Virginia (1779–1781). Just after the war ended, from mid-1784 Jefferson served as a diplomat, stationed in Paris. In May 1785, he became the United States Minister to France. Jefferson was the first United States Secretary of State (1790–

1793) serving under President George Washington. In opposition to Alexander Hamilton's Federalism, Jefferson and his close friend, James Madison, organized the Democratic-Republican Party, and subsequently resigned from Washington's cabinet. Elected Vice President in 1796, when he came in second to President John Adams of the Federalists, Jefferson opposed Adams and with Madison secretly wrote the Kentucky and Virginia Resolutions, which attempted to nullify the Alien and Sedition Acts.

Elected president in what Jefferson called the Revolution of 1800, he oversaw the purchase of the vast Louisiana Territory from France (1803), and sent the Lewis and Clark Expedition (1804–1806) to explore the new west. Jefferson is considered a primary architect of American expansionism; the United States having doubled in size during his presidency. His second term was beset with troubles at home, such as the failed treason trial of his former Vice President Aaron Burr. With escalating trouble with Britain who was challenging American neutrality and threatening shipping at sea, he tried economic warfare with his embargo laws which only damaged American trade. In 1803, President Jefferson initiated a process of Indian tribal removal and relocation to the Louisiana Territory west of the Mississippi River, in order to open lands for eventual American settlers. In 1807, he drafted and signed into law a bill banning the importation of slaves into the United States.

A leader in the Enlightenment, Jefferson was a polymath who spoke five languages and was deeply interested in science, invention, architecture, religion, and philosophy and was an active member and eventual president of the American Philosophical Society. These interests led him to the founding of the University of Virginia after his presidency. He designed his own large mansion on a 5,000-acre plantation near Charlottesville, Virginia, which he named Monticello and the University of Virginia building. While not a notable orator, Jefferson was a skilled writer and corresponded with many influential people in America and Europe throughout his adult life.

STEVEN PAUL "STEVE" JOBS (February 24, 1955 – October 5, 2011) was an American entrepreneur, marketer, and inventor, who was the co-founder (along with Steve Wozniak and Ronald Wayne), chairman, and CEO of Apple Inc. Through Apple, he is widely recognized as a charismatic pioneer of the personal computer revolution and for his influential career in the computer and consumer electron- ics fields, transforming "one industry after another, from computers and Smartphones to music and movies." Jobs also co-founded and served as chief executive of Pixar Animation Studios; he became a member of the board of directors of The Walt Disney Company in 2006, when Disney acquired Pixar. Jobs was among the first to see the commercial potential of Xerox PARC's mouse- driven graphical user interface, which led to the creation of the Apple Lisa and, a year later, the Macintosh. He also played a role in introducing the LaserWriter, one of the first widely available laser printers, to the market.

After a power struggle with the board of directors in 1985, Jobs left Apple and founded NeXT, a computer platform development company specializing in the higher-education and business markets. In 1986, he acquired the computer graphics division of Lucas-film, which was spun off as Pixar. He was credited in Toy Story (1995) as an executive producer. He served as CEO and majority shareholder until Disney's purchase of Pixar in 2006. In 1996, after Apple had failed to deliver its operating system, Copland, Gil Amelio turned to NeXT Computer, and the NeXTSTEP platform became the foundation for the Mac OS X. Jobs returned to Apple as an advisor, and took control of the company as an interim CEO. Jobs brought Apple from near bankruptcy to profitability by 1998.

As the new CEO of the company, Jobs oversaw the development of the iMac, iTunes, iPod, iPhone, and iPad, and on the services side, the company's Apple Retail Stores, iTunes Store and the App Store. The success of these products and services provided several years of stable financial returns, and propelled Apple to become the world's most valuable publicly traded company in 2011. The reinvigoration of the company is regarded by many commentators as one of the greatest turnarounds in business history.

MICHAEL JEFFREY JORDAN (born February 17, 1963), also known by his initials, MJ, is an American former professional basketball player, entrepreneur, and majority owner and chairman of the Charlotte Bobcats. His biography on the National Basketball Association (NBA) website states, "By acclamation, Michael Jordan is the greatest basketball player of all time." Jordan was one of the most effectively marketed athletes of his generation and was considered instrumental in popularizing the NBA around the world in the 1980s and 1990s.

After a three-season career at the University of North Carolina at Chapel Hill, where he was a member of the Tar Heels' national championship team in 1982, Jordan joined the NBA's Chicago Bulls in 1984. He quickly emerged as a league star, entertaining crowds with his prolific scoring. His leaping ability, illustrated by performing slam dunks from the free throw line in slam dunk contests, earned him the nicknames "Air Jordan" and "His Airness". He also gained a reputation for being one of the best defensive players in basketball. In 1991, he won his first NBA championship with the Bulls, and followed that achievement with titles in 1992 and 1993, securing a "three-peat". Although Jordan abruptly retired from basketball before the beginning of the 1993–94 NBA season to pursue a career in baseball, he rejoined the Bulls in 1995 and led them to three additional championships in 1996, 1997, and 1998, as well as an NBA-record 72 regular- season wins in the 1995–96 NBA season. Jordan retired for a second time in 1999, but returned for two more NBA seasons from 2001 to 2003 as a member of the Washington Wizards.

Jordan's individual accolades and accomplishments include five Most Valuable Player (MVP) Awards, ten All-NBA First Team designations, nine All-Defensive First Team honors, fourteen NBA All-Star Game appearances, three All-Star Game MVP Awards, ten scoring titles, three steals titles, six NBA Finals MVP Awards, and the 1988 NBA Defensive Player of the Year Award. Among his numerous accomplishments, Jordan holds the

NBA records for highest career regular season scoring average (30.12 points per game) and highest career playoff scoring average (33.45 points per game). In 1999, he was named the greatest North American athlete of the 20th century by ESPN, and was second to Babe Ruth on the Associated Press's list of athletes of the century. He is a two-time inductee into the Basketball Hall of Fame - in 2009 for his individual career and in 2010 as a member of the 1992 United States men's Olympic basketball team ("The Dream Team").

MARTIN LUTHER KING, JR. (January 15, 1929 – April 4, 1968) was an American pastor, activist, humanitarian, and leader in the African- American Civil Rights Movement. He is best known for his role in the advancement of civil rights using nonviolent civil disobedience based on his Christian beliefs.

He was born Michael King, but his father changed his name in honor of German reformer Martin Luther. A Baptist minister, King became a civil rights activist early in his career. He led the 1955 Montgomery Bus Boycott and helped found the Southern Christian Leadership Conference (SCLC) in 1957, serving as its first president. With the

SCLC, King led an unsuccessful struggle against segregation in Albany, Georgia, in 1962, and organized nonviolent protests in Birmingham, Alabama, that attracted national attention following television news coverage of the brutal police response. King also helped to organize the 1963 March on Washington, where he delivered his "I Have a Dream" speech. There, he established his reputation as one of the greatest orators in American history. J. Edgar Hoover considered him a radical and made him an object of the Federal Bureau of Investigation's COINTELPRO for the rest of his life. FBI agents investigated him for possible communist ties, recorded his extramarital liaisons and reported on them to government officials, and on one occasion, mailed King a threatening anonymous letter which he interpreted as an attempt to make him commit suicide.

On October 14, 1964, King received the Nobel Peace Prize for combating racial inequality through nonviolence. In 1965, he and the SCLC helped to organize the Selma to Montgomery marches and the following year, he took the movement north to Chicago to work on segregated housing. In the final years of his life, King expanded his focus to include poverty and the Vietnam War, alienating many of his liberal allies with a 1967 speech titled "Beyond Vietnam". In 1968 King was planning a national occupation of Washington, D.C., to be called the Poor People's Campaign, when he was assassinated on April 4 in Memphis, Tennessee. His death was followed by riots in many U.S. cities. Allegations that James Earl Ray, the man convicted of killing King, had been framed or acted in concert with government agents persisted for decades after the shooting. The jury of a 1999 civil trial found Loyd Jowers to be complicit in a conspiracy against King.

King was posthumously awarded the Presidential Medal of Freedom and the Congressional Gold Medal. Martin Luther King, Jr. Day was established as a holiday in numerous cities and states beginning in 1971, and as a U.S. federal holiday in 1986. Hundreds of streets and a county in the U.S. have been renamed in his honor. A memorial statue on the National Mall was opened to the public in 2011.

SHELTON JACKSON "SPIKE" LEE (born March 20, 1957) is an American film director, producer, writer, and actor. His production company, 40 Acres and a Mule Filmworks, has produced over 35 films since 1983.

Lee's movies have examined race relations, colorism in the black community, the role of media in contemporary life, urban crime and poverty, and other political issues. Lee has won numerous awards, including an Emmy Award. He has also received two Academy Award nominations Lee's thesis film, *Joe's Bed-Stuy Barbershop: We Cut Heads*, was the first student film to be showcased in Lincoln Center's New Directors New Films Festival.

In 1985, Lee began work on his first feature film, *She's Gotta Have It.* With a budget of $175,000, he shot the film in two weeks. When the film was released in 1986, it grossed over $7,000,000 at the U.S. box office.

Lee's 1989 film *Do the Right Thing* was nominated for an Academy Award for Best Original Screenplay in 1989. Many people, including Hollywood's Kim Basinger believed that *Do the Right Thing* also deserved a Best Picture nomination. Driving Miss Daisy won Best Picture that year. Lee said in an April 7, 2006 interview with New York magazine that the other film's success, which he thought was based on safe stereotypes, hurt him more than if his film had not been nominated for an award.

After the 1990 release of *Mo' Better Blues*, Lee was accused of anti-Semitism by the Anti-

Defamation League and several film critics. They criticized the characters of the club owners Josh and Moe Flatbush, described as "Shylocks". Lee denied the charge, explaining that he wrote those characters in order to depict how black artists struggled against exploitation. Lee said that Lew Wasserman, Sidney Sheinberg or Tom Pollock, the Jewish heads of MCA and Universal Studios, were unlikely to allow anti-Semitic content in a film they produced. He said he could not make an anti-Semitic film because Jews run Hollywood, and "that's a fact."

His 1997 documentary *4 Little Girls*, about the children killed in the 16th Street Baptist Church bombing in Birmingham, Alabama in 1963, was nominated for the Best Feature Documentary Academy Award.

On May 2, 2007, the 50th San Francisco International Film Festival honored Spike Lee with the San Francisco Film Society's Directing Award. He received the 2008 Wexner Prize. In 2013, he won The Dorothy and Lillian Gish Prize, one of the richest prizes in the American arts worth $300,000.

ABRAHAM LINCOLN (February 12, 1809 – April 15, 1865) was the 16th President of the United States, serving from March 1861 until his assassination in April 1865. Lincoln led the United States through its Civil War—its bloodiest war and its greatest moral, constitutional and political crisis. In so doing, he preserved the Union, abolished slavery, strengthened the national government and modernized the economy.

Reared in a poor family on the western frontier, Lincoln was a self-educated lawyer in Illinois, a Whig Party leader, state legislator during the 1830s, and a one-term member of the Congress during the 1840s. He promoted rapid modernization of the economy through banks, canals, railroads and tariffs to encourage the building of factories; he opposed the war with Mexico in 1846. After a series of highly publicized debates in 1858 during which he opposed the expansion of slavery, Lincoln lost the U.S. Senate race to his arch-rival, Democrat Stephen A. Douglas. Lincoln, a moderate from a swing state, secured the Republican Party presidential nomination in 1860. With almost no support in the South, Lincoln swept the North and was elected president in 1860. His election prompted seven southern slave states to form the Confederacy. No compromise or reconciliation was found regarding slavery.

When the North enthusiastically rallied behind the national flag after the Confederate at- tack on Fort Sumter on April 12, 1861, Lincoln concentrated on the military and political dimensions of the war effort. His goal was to reunite the nation. He suspended habeas corpus, arresting and temporarily detaining thousands of suspected secessionists in the Border States without trial. Lincoln averted British intervention by defusing the Trent affair in late 1861. His numerous complex moves toward ending slavery centered on the Emancipation Proclamation in 1863, using the Army to protect escaped slaves, encouraging the border states to outlaw slavery, and helping push through Congress the Thirteenth Amendment to the United States Constitution, which permanently outlawed slavery. Lincoln closely supervised the war effort, especially the selection of top gener- als, including commanding general Ulysses S. Grant. He made the major decisions on Union war strategy, Lincoln's Navy set up a naval blockade that shut down the South's normal trade, helped take control of Kentucky and Tennessee, and gained control of the Southern river system using gunboats. He tried repeatedly to capture the Confederate capital at Richmond. Each time a general failed, Lincoln substituted another until finally Grant succeeded in 1865.

An exceptionally astute politician deeply involved with power issues in each state, Lin- coln reached out to "War Democrats" (who supported the North against the South), and managed his own re-election in the 1864 presidential election. As the leader of the moderate faction of the Republican Party, confronted Radical Republicans who demanded harsher treatment of the South, War Democrats who called for more compromise, Copperheads who despised him, and irreconcilable secessionists who plotted his death. Politically, Lincoln fought back with patronage, by pitting his opponents against each other, and by appealing to the American people with his powers of oratory. His Gettysburg Address of 1863 became an iconic statement of America's dedication to the principles of nationalism, republicanism, equal rights, liberty, and democracy. Lincoln held a moderate view of Reconstruction, seeking to reunite the nation speedily through a policy of generous reconciliation in the face of lingering and bitter divisiveness. Six days after the surrender of Confederate commanding General Robert E. Lee, Lincoln was assassinated by a confederate sympathizer. Lincoln has been consistently ranked both by scholars and the public as one of the greatest U.S. presidents.

NELSON ROLIHLAHLA MANDELA (July 1918 – December 5, 2013) was a South African anti-apartheid revolutionary, politician, and philanthropist who served as President of South Africa from 1994 to 1999. He was South Africa's first black chief executive, and the first elected in a fully representative democratic election. His government focused on dismantling the legacy of apartheid through tackling institutionalized racism, poverty and inequality, and fostering racial reconciliation. Politically an African nationalist and democratic socialist, he served as President of the African National Congress (ANC) from 1991 to 1997. Internationally, Mandela was Secretary General of the Non-Aligned Movement from 1998 to 1999.

A Xhosa born to the Thembu royal family, Mandela attended the Fort Hare University and the University of Witwatersrand, where he studied law. Living in Johannesburg, he became involved in anti-colonial politics, joining the ANC and becoming a founding member of its Youth League. After the South African National Party came to power in 1948, he rose to prominence in the ANC's 1952 Defiance Campaign, was appointed superintendent of the organization's Transvaal chapter and presided over the 1955

Congress of the People. Working as a lawyer, he was repeatedly arrested for seditious activities and, with the ANC leadership, was unsuccessfully prosecuted in the Treason Trial from 1956 to 1961. Influenced by Marxism, he secretly joined the South African Communist Party (SACP) and sat on its Central Committee. Although initially commit- ted to non-violent protest, in association with the SACP he co-founded the militant Umkhonto we Sizwe (MK) in 1961, leading a sabotage campaign against the apartheid government. In 1962, he was arrested, convicted of conspiracy to overthrow the state, and sentenced to life imprisonment in the Rivonia Trial.

Mandela served over 27 years in prison, initially on Robben Island, and later in Pollsmoor Prison and Victor Verster Prison. An international campaign lobbied for his release. He was released in 1990, during a time of escalating civil strife. Mandela joined negotiations with President F. W. de Klerk to abolish apartheid and establish multiracial elections in 1994, in which he led the ANC to victory and became South Africa's first black president. He published his autobiography in 1995. During his tenure in the Government of National Unity, he invited several other political parties to join the cabinet. As agreed to during the negotiations to end apartheid in South Africa, he promulgated a new constitution. He also created the Truth and Reconciliation Commission to investigate past human rights abuses. While continuing the former government's liberal economic policy, his administration also introduced measures to encourage land reform, combat poverty, and expand healthcare services. Internationally, he acted as mediator between Libya and the United Kingdom in the Pan Am Flight 103 bombing trial, and oversaw military intervention in Lesotho. He declined to run for a second term, and was succeeded by his deputy, Thabo Mbeki. Mandela became an elder statesman, focusing on charitable work in combating poverty and HIV/AIDS through the Nelson Mandela Foundation.

Mandela was a controversial figure for much of his life. Denounced as a communist terrorist by critics, he nevertheless gained international acclaim for his activism, having received more than 250 honors, including the 1993 Nobel Peace Prize, the US Presidential Medal of Freedom, the Soviet Order of Lenin and the Bharat Ratna. He is held in deep respect within South Africa, where he is often referred to by his Xhosa clan name, Madiba, or as Tata ("Father"); he is often described as "the father of the nation".

JOHN C. MAXWELL was born in Garden City, Michigan in 1947. Religiously, he is an evangelical Christian. He followed his father into the ministry, completing a bachelor's degree at Ohio Christian University in 1969, a Master of Divinity degree at Azusa Pacific University, and a Doctor of Ministry degree at Fuller Theological Seminary. He currently resides in South Florida with his wife, Margaret.

For over 30 years, Maxwell has led churches in Indiana, Ohio, California, and Florida. After serving as senior pastor for 14 years, in 1995 he left Skyline Church to devote himself full-time to speaking and writing. However, in 2004, he returned to congregational ministry at Christ Fellowship in Palm Beach Gardens, Florida, where he is currently a teaching pastor. On November 16, 2008, he began serving as a guest pastor at the famous Crystal Cathedral in Orange County, California. Maxwell's mentor, Robert H. Schuller, has had a variety of noted evangelical pastors preach at his mega church since his son, Robert A. Schuller, resigned as senior pastor in 2008. Maxwell has returned to preach at the Crystal Cathedral several times and his messages are broadcast on the Hour of Power television program.

Maxwell is an internationally recognized leadership expert, speaker, and author. He is the founder of INJOY, Maximum Impact, ISS and EQUIP, an international leadership development organization working to help leaders. EQUIP is involved with leaders from more than 80 nations. Its mission is "to see effective Christian leaders fulfill the Great Commission in every nation."

Every year Maxwell speaks to Fortune 500 companies, international government leaders, and organizations as diverse as the United States Military Academy at West Point and the National Football League. A New York Times, Wall Street Journal, and Business Week best-selling author, Maxwell was one of 25 authors named to Amazon.com's 10th Anniversary Hall of Fame. Three of his books, The 21 Irrefutable Laws of Leadership, Developing the Leader Within You, and The 21 Indispensable Qualities of a Leader have each sold over a million copies.

Maxwell serves on the Board of Trustees at Indiana Wesleyan University and has a building named after him there, the Maxwell Center for Business and Leadership. Max- well was a keynote speaker at National Agents Alliance NAA Leadership Conference several times most recently in 2010.] In 2012, he was awarded the Golden Gavel by Toastmasters International.

JOYCE MEYER (born Pauline Joyce Hutchison; June 4, 1943) is a Charismatic Christian author and speaker. Meyer and her husband Dave have four grown children, and live outside St. Louis, Missouri. Her ministry is headquartered in the St. Louis suburb of Fenton, Missouri. Meyer speaks humorously, sharing with her audience her own short-comings and taking playful jabs at stereotypical church behavior. A particular crowd favorite is the "robot" routine, in which she goes into a stiff-armed imitation of a robot chanting "What about me? What about me?"

According to Joyce Meyer Ministries, Meyer earned her doctoral degree from Life Christian University, an unaccredited institution in Tampa, Florida. Meyer has been given an Honorary Doctorate of Divinity by Oral Roberts University, an accredited institution in Tulsa, Oklahoma.

DR. MYLES MUNROE (April 20, 1954 - Nov. 9, 2014)) was the president and founder of the Bahamas Faith Ministries International (BFMI) and Myles Munroe International (MMI), a Christian growth and resource

center that includes leadership training institutes, a missions agency, a publishing company, a television network, radio and web communications, and a church community. He was chief executive officer and chairman of the board of the International Third World Leaders Association and president of the International Leadership Training Institute. He was the author of 23 books and was a motivational speaker.

Myles Munroe was born in Nassau, Bahamas in 1954 and was a lifetime resident of the Bahamas. He had degrees in fine arts, education and theology from Oral Roberts University (1978), a Master's degree in administration from the University of Tulsa (1980), and he was awarded a number of honorary doctoral degrees. He was also served as an adjunct professor of the Graduate School of Theology at Oral Roberts University. His wife, Ruth Munroe (who passed away with him in a tragic jet crash in Freeport Bahamas) was co pastor with him at BFMI. He has a son Chairo (Myles Jr.) and daughter Charisa and said that his family is his greatest responsibility and his marriage his most sacred trust.

During his later years, Dr. Munroe was a pastor, teacher, administrator, author, a father, a husband and motivational speaker. He traveled throughout the world as a speaker addressing government leaders, businesses, schools/universities and church congregations. He personally addressed over 500,000 people each year on personal and professional development, and he received hundreds of invitations every year to speak worldwide. Dr. Munroe has appeared on Pastor Benny Hinn's This Is Your Day program, where he spoke about the Kingdom of God.

Dr. Munroe always placed an emphasis on the Kingdom of God and believes that the whole Bible, along with the message of Jesus, revolved around the kingdom and not a religion. He said, "My vision, is wrapped up in one statement: I exist to transform followers into leaders. My philosophy is, trapped in every follower is a leader. My belief is, if that person is placed in the right environment, the leader will manifest himself or herself."

RICHARD MILHOUS NIXON (January 9, 1913 – April 22, 1994) was the 37th President of the United States, serving from 1969 to 1974, when he became the only president to resign the office. Nixon had previously served as a U.S. Representative and Senator from California and as the 36th Vice President of the United States from 1953 to 1961.

Nixon was born in Yorba Linda, California. He graduated from Whittier College in 1934 and Duke University School of Law in 1937, returning to California to practice law. He and his wife, Pat Nixon, moved to Washington to work for the federal government in 1942. He subsequently served in the United States Navy during World War II. Nixon was elected in California to the House of Representatives in 1946 and to the Senate in 1950. His pursuit of the Alger Hiss case established his reputation as a leading anti-communist, and elevated him to national prominence. He was the running mate of Dwight D. Eisenhower, the Republican Party presidential nominee in the 1952 election. Nixon served for eight years as vice president. He waged an unsuccessful presidential campaign in 1960, narrowly losing to John F. Kennedy, and lost a race for Governor of California in 1962. In 1968, he ran again for the presidency and was elected.

Although Nixon initially escalated America's involvement in the Vietnam War, he subsequently ended U.S. involvement by 1973. Nixon's visit to the People's Republic of China in 1972 opened communications between the two nations and eventually led to the normalization of diplomatic relations. He initiated détente and the Anti-Ballistic Missile Treaty with the Soviet Union the same year. Domestically, his administration generally embraced policies that transferred power from

Washington to the states. Among other things, he launched initiatives to fight cancer and illegal drugs, imposed wage and price controls, enforced desegregation of Southern schools, implemented environmental re- forms, and introduced legislation to reform healthcare and welfare. Though he presided over the lunar landings beginning with Apollo 11, he replaced manned space exploration with shuttle missions. He was re-elected by a landslide in 1972.

Nixon's second term saw a crisis in the Middle East, resulting in an oil embargo and the restart of the Middle East peace process, as well as a continuing series of revelations about the Watergate scandal. The scandal escalated, costing Nixon much of his political support, and on August 9, 1974, he resigned in the face of almost certain impeachment and removal from office. After his resignation, he accepted a pardon issued by his successor, Gerald Ford. In retirement, Nixon's work as an elder statesman, authoring nine books and undertaking many foreign trips, helped to rehabilitate his public image. He suffered a debilitating stroke on April 18, 1994, and died four days later at the age of 81.

JOEL SCOTT OSTEEN (born March 5, 1963) is an American preacher, televangelist, author, and the Senior Pastor of Lakewood Church, the largest church in the United States, in Houston, Texas. His ministry is seen by over 7 million broadcast media viewers weekly and over 20 million monthly in over 100 nations around the world. Osteen has written five New York Times Bestselling books. He has been widely nicknamed "The Smiling Preacher".

In 2004, his first book, Your Best Life Now, was released by Time Warner and debuted at the top of the The New York Times Best Seller list. The book remained The New York Times Bestseller for more than 200 weeks and has sold more than 4 million copies. His next four books, Become a Better You, It's Your Time, Every Day A Friday, and I Declare, have all also been #1 national bestsellers.

TYLER PERRY (born Emmitt Perry, Jr.; September 13, 1969) is an American actor, director, screenwriter, playwright, producer, author, and songwriter, specializing in the gospel genre. Perry wrote and produced many stage plays during the 1990s

and early 2000s. In 2011, Forbes named him the highest paid man in entertainment; he earned $130 million between May 2010 and 2011.

Perry is known for both creating and performing in drag the Madea character, a giant, over reactive, and thuggishly tough elderly woman. Perry also creates films, some produced as live recordings of stage plays, and others professionally filmed using full sets and locations with full editing. Perry is estimated to have earned around $75 million by 2008. Many of Perry's stage-play films have been subsequently adapted as professional films.

Perry has also created several television shows, his most successful of which is Tyler Perry's House of Payne, a show that ran for eight seasons on TBS from June 21, 2006, to August 10, 2012. On October 2, 2012, Perry struck an exclusive multi-year partnership with Oprah Winfrey and her Oprah Winfrey Network. The partnership was largely for the purposes of bringing scripted television to the OWN network, Perry having had previous success in this department. To date, Perry has created two original series for the network, The Haves and the Have Nots and Love Thy Neighbor. The Haves and The Have Nots has supplied OWN with very successful ratings and has also been critically acclaimed as being "one of OWN's biggest success stories

GRANVILLE "ORAL" ROBERTS (January 24, 1918 – December 15, 2009) was an American Methodist–Pentecostal televangelist and a Christian charismatic. He founded the Oral Roberts Evangelistic Association and Oral Roberts University.

As one of the most well-known and controversial American religious leaders of the 20th century, Roberts preached a form of Christianity he called seed-faith. His ministries reached millions of followers worldwide spanning a period of over six decades. His healing ministry and bringing American Pentecostalism into the mainstream had the most impact, but he also pioneered TV evangelism and laid the foundations of the prosperity gospel and abundant life teachings.

JACK ROOSEVELT "JACKIE" ROBINSON (January 31, 1919 – October 24, 1972) was an American baseball player who became the first African-American to play in Major League Baseball (MLB) in the modern era. Robinson broke the baseball color line when the Brooklyn Dodgers started him at first base on April

15, 1947. As the first major league team to play a black man since the 1880s, the Dodgers ended racial segregation that had relegated black players to the Negro leagues for six decades. The example of Robinson's character and unquestionable talent challenged the traditional basis of segregation, which then marked many other aspects of American life, and contributed significantly to the Civil Rights Movement.

In addition to his cultural impact, Robinson had an exceptional baseball career. Over 10 seasons, Robinson played in six World Series and contributed to the Dodgers' 1955 World Championship. He was selected for six consecutive All-Star Games, from 1949 to 1954, was the recipient of the inaugural MLB Rookie of the Year Award in 1947, and won the National League Most Valuable Player Award in 1949 — the first black player so honored. Robinson was inducted into the Baseball Hall of Fame in 1962. In 1997, Major League Baseball "universally" retired his uniform number, 42, across all major league teams; he was the first pro athlete in any sport to be so honored. Initiated for the first time on April 15, 2004, Major League Baseball has adopted a new annual tradition, "Jackie Robinson Day", on which every player on every team wears #42.

Robinson was also known for his pursuits outside the baseball diamond. He was the first black television analyst in MLB, and the first black vice president of a major American corporation. In the 1960s, he helped establish the Freedom National Bank, an African-American-owned financial institution based in Harlem, New York. In recognition of his achievements on and off the field, Robinson was posthumously awarded the Presidential Medal of Freedom and the Congressional Gold Medal.

BRIAN TRACY is Chairman and CEO of Brian Tracy International, a company specializing in the training and development of individuals and organizations.

Brian's goal is to help people achieve their personal and business goals faster and easier than they ever imagined.

Brian Tracy has consulted for more than 1,000 companies and addressed more than 5,000,000 people in 5,000 talks and seminars throughout the US, Canada and 55 other countries worldwide. As a Keynote speaker and seminar leader, he addresses more than 250,000 people each year.

He has studied, researched, written and spoken for 30 years in the fields of economics, history, business, philosophy and psychology. He is the top selling author of over 45 books that have been translated into dozens of languages.

He has written and produced more than 300 audio and video learning programs, including the worldwide, best-selling Psychology of Achievement, which has been translated into more than 20 languages.

He speaks to corporate and public audiences on the subjects of Personal and Professional Development, including the executives and staff of many of America's largest corporations. His exciting talks and seminars on Leadership, Selling, Self-Esteem, Goals, Strategy, Creativity and Success Psychology bring about immediate changes and long- term results. (content taken from BrianTracy.com)

BOOKER TALIAFERRO WASHINGTON (April 5, 1856 – November 14, 1915) was an African-American educator, author, orator, and advisor to presidents of the United States. Between 1890 and 1915, Washington was the dominant leader in the African-American community.

Washington was of the last generation of black American leaders born into slavery and became the leading voice of the former slaves and their descendants, who were newly oppressed by disfranchisement and the Jim Crow discriminatory laws enacted in the post-Reconstruction Southern states in the late 19th and early 20th centuries. In 1895, his Atlanta compromise called for avoiding confrontation over segregation and instead putting more reliance on long-term educational and economic advancement in the black community.

His base was the Tuskegee Institute, a historically black college in Alabama. As lynchings in the South reached a peak in 1895, Washington gave a speech in Atlanta that made him nationally famous. The speech called for black progress through education and entrepreneurship. His message was that it was not the time to challenge Jim Crow segregation and the disfranchisement of black voters in the South. Washington mobilized a nationwide coalition of middle-class blacks, church leaders, and white philanthropists and politicians, with a long-term goal of building the community's economic strength and pride by a focus on self-help and schooling. Secretly, he supported court challenges to segregation. Black militants in the North, led by W.E.B. DuBois, at first supported the Atlanta Compromise but after 1909 they set up the NAACP and tried with little success to challenge Washington's political machine for leadership in the black community. Decades after Washington's death in 1915, the Civil Rights movement generally moved away from his policies to take the more militant NAACP approach.

Booker T. Washington mastered the nuances of the political arena in the late 19th century which enabled him to manipulate the media, raise money, strategize, network, pressure, reward friends and distribute funds while punishing those who opposed his plans for uplifting blacks. His long-term goal was to end the disfranchisement of the vast majority of African Americans living in southern states, where most of the millions of black Americans still lived.

HAROLD WASHINGTON (born Harold Lee Washington) (April 15, 1922 – November 25, 1987) was an American lawyer, politician and elected in 1983 as the 51st Mayor of Chicago. He was the first African-American Mayor of Chicago, serving from 1983 until his death in 1987. He was also a member of the U.S. House of Representatives from 1981 to 1983 representing the Illinois first district, and also previously served in the Illinois State Senate and the Illinois House of Representatives.

In the February 22, 1983, Democratic mayoral primary, community organizers registered more than 100,000 new African American, Latino and poor and independent white voters, while the white vote was split between the incumbent mayor Jane Byrne and future mayor Richard M. Daley, son of the late Mayor Richard J. Daley. Washington won with 37% of the vote, versus 33% for Byrne and 30% for Daley.

Although winning the Democratic primary is normally tantamount to election in heavily Democratic Chicago, after his primary victory Washington found that his Republican opponent, former state legislator Bernard Elton (earlier considered a nominal stand-in), was supported by many white Democrats and ward organizations, including the chairman of the Cook County Democratic Party, Alderman Edward "Fast Eddie" Vrdolyak Epton's campaign referred to, among other things, Washington's conviction for failure to file income tax returns. (He had paid the taxes, but had not filed a return.) However, Washington appealed to his constituency in his mayoral political campaign, and stressed such things as reforming the Chicago patronage system and the need for a jobs program in a tight economy. In the April 12, 1983, mayoral general election,

Washington defeated Epton by 3.7%, 51.7% to 48.0%, to become mayor of Chicago. Washington was sworn in as mayor on April 29, 1983, and resigned his Congressional seat the following day.

During his tenure as mayor, Washington lived at the Hampton House apartments in the Hyde Park neighborhood of Chicago. Among the changes he made to the city's government was creating its first environmental-affairs department under the management of longtime Great Lakes environmentalist Lee Botts. Washington's victory marked the end of race lines, such as Western Avenue in Chicago Lawn, which had kept black Americans from living in white neighborhoods. Washington's first term in office was characterized by ugly, racially polarized battles dubbed "Council Wars", referring to the then-recent Star Wars films. A 29–21 City Council majority refused to enact Washington's reform legislation and prevented him from appointing reform nominees to boards and commissions.

OPRAH GAIL WINFREY (born January 29, 1954) is an American media proprietor, talk show host, actress, producer, and philanthropist. Winfrey is best known for her multi-award-winning talk show The Oprah Winfrey Show which was the highest-rated program of its kind in history and was nationally syndicated from 1986 to 2011. Dubbed the "Queen of All Media" she has been ranked the richest African-American of the 20th century, the greatest black philanthropist in American history, and is currently North America's only black billionaire. She is also, according to some assessments, the most influential woman in the world. In 2013, she was awarded the Presidential Medal of Freedom by President Barack Obama and an honorary doctorate degree from Harvard.

Winfrey was born into poverty in rural Mississippi to a teenage single mother and later raised in an inner-city Milwaukee neighborhood. She experienced considerable hard- ship during her childhood, saying she was raped at age nine and became pregnant at 14; her son died in infancy. Sent to live with the man she calls her father, a barber in Tennessee, Winfrey landed a job in radio while still in high school and began co-anchoring the local evening news at the age of 19. Her emotional ad-lib delivery eventually got her transferred to the daytime-talk-show arena, and after boosting a third-rated local Chicago talk show to first place, she launched her own production company and became internationally syndicated.

Credited with creating a more intimate confessional form of media communication, she is thought to have popularized and revolutionized the tabloid talk show genre pioneered by Phil Donahue, which a Yale study says broke 20th-century taboos. By the mid- 1990s, she had reinvented her show with a focus on literature, self-improvement, and spirituality. Though criticized for unleashing a confession culture, promoting controversial self-help ideas, and an emotion-centered approach she is often praised for overcoming adversity to become a benefactor to others.

DR. WILLIAM "BILL" WINSTON, Born in Tuskegee, Alabama, Dr. Winston was inspired and influenced for leadership by the abundance of educators, scientists, and physicians who surrounded him as a youth, and by the historic aviation accomplishments of the Tuskegee Airmen who served as his role models. He is a graduate of the internationally known Tuskegee Institute in Tuskegee, Alabama (now Tuskegee University), where Booker T. Washington's and George Washington Carver's legacies of leadership and invention permeated the environment.

Dr. Winston served for six years as a fighter pilot in the United States Air Force, where his extraordinary achievement in aerial flight earned him The Distinguished Flying Cross, The Air Medal for performance in combat, and the Squadron Top Gun Award.

After completing his military service, Dr. Winston joined the IBM Corporation as a marketing representative. His exceptional managerial and relational skills rapidly earned him several promotions within the organization. Before he resigned in 1985 to enter full-time ministry, he was a regional marketing manager in IBM's Midwest Region.

He is the founder and pastor of Living Word Christian Center, a multi-cultural, non-denominational church with more than 20,000 members located in Forest Park, Illinois. The church has a broad range of ministries and related entities.

Dr. Winston is also the founder of the Joseph Business School (JBS) and The Joseph Center® for Business Development for entrepreneurs and business leaders. JBS is located in Forest Park, Illinois with eleven other partnership locations across the U.S. and internationally. The Joseph Business School also has an online E-Learning program.

Dr. Winston is also the founder of Bill Winston Ministries (BWM), a partnership-based outreach ministry. Through BWM, he hosts the Believer's Walk of Faith television and radio broadcast which reaches more than 800 million households nationwide and overseas.

Dr. Winston's ministry owns and operates two shopping malls and Golden Eagle Aviation, a fixed-based operation located on historic Moton Field in Tuskegee, Alabama. (information taken from BillWinston.org)

HILARY HINTON "ZIG" ZIGLAR (November 6, 1926 – November 28, 2012) was an American author, salesman, and motivational speaker. Zig Ziglar was born in Coffee County in southeastern Alabama to parents John Silas Ziglar and Lila Wescott Ziglar. He was the tenth of twelve children.

In 1931, when Ziglar was five years old, his father took a management position at a Mississippi farm, and his family moved to Yazoo City, Mississippi, where he spent most of his early childhood. The next year, his father died of a stroke, and his younger sister died two days later.

Ziglar served in the United States Navy during

World War II, from 1943 to 1945. He was in the Navy V-12 Navy College Training Program and attended the University of South Carolina in Columbia, South Carolina.

In 1944, he met his wife, Jean, in the capital city of Mississippi, Jackson; he was seven- teen and she was sixteen. They married in late 1946.
Ziglar later worked as a salesman in a succession of companies. In 1968, he became a vice president and training director for the Automotive Performance Company, moving to Dallas, Texas.

As of 2010, Ziglar still traveled around taking part in motivational seminars, despite a fall down a flight of stairs in 2007 that left him with short-term memory problems. State Representative Chris Greeley of Maine mentions Ziglar in the credits of his CD on public speaking. Ziglar wove his Christianity into his motivational work. He was also an open Republican who endorsed former Governor Mike Huckabee for his party's presidential nomination in 2008.

Biography Index

Alphabetical Order: Chapter, Reference page number

John Avanzini, Chapter 2 p.55

Wade Boggs, Chapter 4 p.91

Kobe Bryant, Chapter 2 p.68

George Washington Carver, Chapter 1 p.12

Raymond Chandler, Chapter 4 p.91

Jesus Christ, Introduction p.xvi; Chapter 1 p.28, 46, 47; Chapter 4 p.93, 94, 103; Chapter 5 p.119; Say Something p.136,137

Winston Churchill, Chapter 4 p.94

Frederick Douglas, Chapter 1 p.12

Charles Drew, Chapter 1 p.12

Thomas Edison, Chapter 3 p.75

Mohandas Gandhi, p.xvii

William Gates, Chapter 1 p.12

Berry Gordy, Jr., Chapter 3 p.83

William Graham, Jr., Chapter 4 p.92

LeBron James, Chapter 2 p.68

Thomas Jefferson, Chapter 4 p.99; Chapter 6 p.132

Steve Jobs, Chapter 1 p.12; Chapter 5 p.65

Michael Jordan, Chapter 1 p.12; Chapter 2 p67,68; Chapter 4 p.100; Chapter 5 pp.114,115

Martin Luther King, Jr., p.xvii; Chapter 1 p.12; Chapter 4 pp.103,104

Spike Lee, Chapter 1 p.12

Abraham Lincoln, p.xvi, xvii; Chapter 4 p.93, 103

Nelson Mandela, p.xvii; Chapter 4 pp.93, 103

John Maxwell, Chapter 4 pp.95, 103

Joyce Meyer, Chapter 5 pp.113,114

Myles Monroe, Chapter 5 p.122

Richard Nixon, Chapter 5 p.115

Joel Osteen, Chapter 4 p.91

Tyler Perry, Chapter 1 p.12

Granville Roberts, Chapter 3 p.84

Jackie Robinson, Chapter 4 pp.93,103

Brian Tracy, Chapter 4 p.92

Booker T. Washington, Chapter 1 p.12

Harold Washington, Chapter 1 p.40; p.202

Oprah Winfrey, Chapter 1 p.12

William Winston, Chapter 1 p.12; Chapter 2 pp. 56,65; Chapter 4 p.93, 103

Zig Ziglar, Chapter 4 p.92

Biographies were adapted by permission from Wikipedia.org unless otherwise noted.

About the Author

Born and raised on the Westside of Chicago, Tarvies D. Smith, Sr. had to learn endurance and perseverance after the death of his parents as a pre-teen. As a result of the lack of parental guidance, structure, vision and personal accountability; Tarvies became angry, frustrated and unmotivated regarding his future.

Tarvies attended middle school at J. Sterling Morton Elementary and later attend John Marshall Metro High School. While attending Marshall, Tarvies began to make change for the better. His aunt received him into her home and provided emotional and mental stability. The love, support and encouragement that was provided by his aunt helped to propel and foster a winning attitude that manifested into the following academic achievements: Top 5% of his graduating senior class, Member of National Honor Society, Member of John Hope Franklin Club, Principal Scholars Program, Recipient of the late Mayor Harold Washington Mercantile Exchange Scholarship Award, Homecoming King and many other academic and personal accomplishments.

After graduating from high school, Tarvies attended Eastern Illinois University (EIU). While attending EIU, Tarvies became a member of Phi

Beta Sigma Fraternity, Inc., and completed his Bachelors Degree in Psychology. Tarvies simultaneous obtained his Masters Degree in Political Science /Public Administration while working for Eastern Student Housing Department as a Hall Counselor.

However, the single most significant personal accomplishment for Tarvies was receiving Jesus Christ as his personal Lord and Savior. Tarvies received his call into the ministry and completed his ministerial training at Living Word Christian Center's Bible Training Center where Tarvies is a current member under the leadership of Dr. Bill Winston. Tarvies obtained his second Master's Degree from Concordia University in School Counseling and graduate of The Joseph Business School and Entrepreneurial Program.

Tarvies' professional work experience includes the following: Supervisory, Program-Management, Social Worker with the Department of Children and Family Services (DCFS), Prevention Specialist, Youth Development Specialist, Motivational Speakers, Author, Mentor, Academic/Career Counselor, Domestic Violence Advocate / Counselor, Community and Family Counselor, Life Coach, Substance Abuse, and Professional School Counselor. Tarvies is the President & CEO of Teen-Train, Inc. which is a Not-For Profit, 501c3 Organization with emphasis on the following services: Academic Enrichment, Career Education, Mentoring Services, Youth & Leadership Development.

Tarvies has membership in the following professional/national organizations:

- American School Counselor Association (ASCA)

- Illinois Counseling Association (ICA)

- Illinois Mental Health Counseling Association (IMHCA)

- Phi Beta Sigma Fraternity, Inc.

Tarvies is married to Tannita Smith and the father of five sons: Tarvies Jr. and Timothy Smith, Josh, Jeremiah, and Jonathan Rabb.